"This is story telling at its best. Betty has given identity to the women of the Bible, some who were mentioned by name and many who were not. As she tells the story, they come alive and with this identity, we can relate to each and every one as if they were among us today. Their stories are not unlike our own. This is a book that should be given space on everyone's book shelf."

Nancy Sutherland, President of the National United Church Women.

"Story teller, Betty Turcott, has used her imagination to bring the reader inside the lives of women of the Bible. People of every age will be able to identify with Betty's characters. The three questions at the end of each story will spark lively discussion, encouraging the reader to apply the experiences in the story to their daily lives. This book is a wonderful resource for Bible study, programs for women's groups and storytellers."

Rev. Janet Stobie, Inspirational Speaker and author of *Dipping Your Toes, Can I hold Him?* and *Fireweed*, www.janetstobie.com

"How refreshing in our hero-worship culture to celebrate stories told from the perspective of the ordinary person on the fringes, where biblical women are often found. Betty has a unique flare for infusing scripture with more meaning and depth by giving voice to these muted women. My favourite is the poignant tale of Delora, imagined mother of Judas. That this reviled man had a loving mother who agonized over her son was a revelation. In the end Delora seeks comfort and support saying, 'Women are wise and they can help me to understand.' I feel the same way about Betty!"

The Reverend Doctor Larry Doyle, B.Mus, B.Ed., M.Div., D.Min.

Other Books by Betty Radford Turcott

Songs for the Journey: Selected Poems, 1993, Women's Inter-Church Council of Canada

There Is a Season: Meditations for Private and Group Worship, 1996, The United Church Publishing House

Follow Me: Meditations for Private and Group Worship, 1999, The United Church Publishing House

Beside Still Waters: Meditations for Private and Group Worship, 2004, The United Church Publishing House

And She Said

Monologues on Biblical Women

Betty Radford Turcott

Published by:
Kentisbeare Press
87 Waverley Rd.,
Bowmanville, ON
L1C 1L2

Photos of Betty by Jim Ellis
Cover Design by Erin Minács

ISBN 978-0-9959905-0-0

10 9 8 7 6 5 4 3 2 1

And She Said

Monologues on Biblical Women

Betty Radford Turcott

This book is dedicated to

The great world-wide sisterhood of women
who have challenged, affirmed and shared my journey;
too many to name but all held in deep affection.

Contents

Chapter 3: Nameless Women

Chapter 4: Women Near the Manger

Chapter 5: Women Who Knew Jesus

Chapter 6: Women Near the Cross

Chapter 7: Women in the Early Church

Forward

This is such a great honour, and humbling, to be asked to offer this forward for my dear friend Betty Turcott. I first met Betty in 1997 so it has been twenty years through which we have shared women's stories, our stories, biblical stories, and joined in faith and friendship together. Betty is a talented writer, a gifted theologian, a thorough researcher and creative revealer of biblical women and their voices. I know these things of Betty because over the years our lunches and chats have sometimes been four hours long. That's a lot of talking as I have been treated to sharing time with Betty and as she has brought her woman's sacred imagination to the ancient scripture stories, stories we need to hear and share.

This book, *And She Said*, invites us, you and me, into the stories of women, their perspectives, their journeys, their challenges and celebrations in life. And this in turn touches our hearts, our minds and our souls as we find ourselves, our stories, entwined in theirs.

Betty gives names and voices to the women in the scriptures, lifting them up from the shadows to be seen and heard. She offers us the life stories of Sarah, Shiprah and Puah, Anna in the Temple, the Bent-Over Woman, and Eunice, just to name a few. Betty introduces us to women whose names mean hope, wisdom, pain and sorrow, friend, ornament, and rejoice. These women demonstrate courage, strength, trust, compassion and faith just as many women have always done.

Over the years, I have read and introduced women in my pastoral charges to Betty's other books. The United Church Women in those churches and many others have used her books to lead them spiritually in meetings and small groups, bringing them closer to each other and to God. I have been at interfaith events and met those from other Christian traditions who have found Betty's books and discovered how they speak to women and men too.

As I read through this literary gift, I found myself comforted by the continuous presence of God on each page, the sacredness and holiness of each woman, the wisdom of women and Love's power that flows to and through each of them. This power, this grace, is what flows to and through each of us, through you and me. Betty's goal is to help us to identify, in what is perhaps only a woman's way, with the story and people involved. I have. May you also feel the invitation to your heart to connect with the woman of the past with whom your story resonates and know that as we continue to share our very sacred and holy women's stories, we join our names and voices to those of the past, through time, and forever.

Thank you, Betty, for this honour, this gift, my wise, caring, holy, and cherished friend.

Rev. Deb Foster, BA(hon), MDiv, ThM
March 6th, 2017.

Introduction
Betty Radford Turcott

At age twelve I had a Sunday School teacher who loved contests. Each week we had to find in the Bible, the names of birds, rivers, city or mountains, and make a list. One week I asked why we never had to find women's names. She liked the idea and that was our challenge for the next week. That week I wrote down the name of every woman I found and added the scripture reference and a sentence about her. That began a life-long interest in these women who lived so many centuries ago.

Two theologians whom I admire and avidly read their works are Rosemary Radford Ruether and Elizabeth Schussler-Fiorenza. From Ruether I learned to look for the voice that was missing from the biblical story and from Schussler-Fiorenza that women need to bring their sacred imaginations to the material. That is what I try to do as I read and think about the women who are mentioned in the Biblical text. All these monologues begin with the Biblical text, but beyond the information given in the Bible, the monologues themselves are creative fiction.

Many of the women in biblical material are not

named. Everyone likes to be called by her name. One way to dismiss a person is to never refer to her by name. I have chosen an Hebrew name for each of these women in the Bible. The meaning of the name in some way reflects their story or some facet of their personality as I have imagined it.

I begin with the text from the Bible and read it a number of times. On the last time I am looking for the missing story behind the written story. Studying life in those times and locations is the second part of my research along with the historical setting. Then comes the reading I do from those who have studied theology. Next I bring my experience as a woman to the story and let my sacred imagination fill in the missing woman and her place in the story.

I approach each re-telling seriously, always doing my best to stay faithful to the intent of the story, but adding my woman's perspective. I first told one of the stories publicly in 1982. It was well received by the audience of about three hundred women. Since then, these stories have been told to groups of two or three in someone's living room, to twenty or thirty in a church basement, or to hundreds in a large auditorium. My goal is to help the listeners identify, in what is perhaps a woman's way, with the story and the people involved.

That is my purpose for this book. It can be used as a personal meditation or reflection guide, or as a tool to study the Bible in groups. If someone is reading the material aloud to a group, she should have read it often enough that she is so familiar with it that she can look at the listeners to help engage them in the story.

The scripture references and the background paragraph, are mainly for the facilitator in a group situation and do not always need to be read. If it would be helpful, the Bible passage noted could be read, or summarized if it is very long. The leader would need to have some knowledge of the amount of familiarity the group has with the Bible to make this decision.

If there is discussion, it is important that each voice be heard and accepted. There are rarely right or wrong answers. Bishop Hannah Faal-Helm said that scripture means what it means for you at the moment of contemplation on the words you read. Respect must be given to each one's life journey.

Chapter 1
Women of the
Hebrew Scriptures

Who Were They

These writings, from which I draw the bare bones of these stories, are referred to as the Hebrew Scriptures and also the Old Testament. They contain ancient stories passed down orally for many generations. They were not written for the purpose of telling the stories of the women who were a part of the life of the people. The fact that women are included in these patriarchal stories attests to the importance of their role in the story of the development of their nation.

Their stories challenge us to confront injustice where ever we find it. It is a fact of history that the gains women have made in one era, country or domain, can be taken away at the stroke of a pen. From these women we learn to be strong, courageous, convinced of our worth and ready to challenge unjust laws and practices.

While their life style differed from ours in so many ways, we share with them many elements of daily life. Their lives contain many events that touch our own at significant moments: changing culture, marriage customs, legal rights, child birth, religious practices and death.

As women, we give birth in many ways, such as finding new paths when the old ones lead us astray. We fight for justice and equality; we teach the young and carry on the traditions of our past. We love, we struggle, we are afraid, and we live in hope for tomorrow.

So did these women, our ancient sisters.

Sarah

Genesis 11:27-32, 12

Background

Ur was the heart of a sophisticated culture. Sarah and Abraham would have lived there during the very height of its power and affluence. The city government was a theocracy under the Babylonian moon god. A number of people understood god in a new way, and Sarah and Abraham were among this group.

* * *

I grew up in the great city of Ur where I was born and I was surrounded by the love of my family. I married Abraham when we were young and I expected to live my life there and be buried with my mother and my grandmother. But it was not to be.

Abraham received a summons from God to go to a new land, far away from our roots and family. I was heart-broken to leave behind all that I had known and loved. But I had no choice and so I began to prepare for the journey and my new and unknown life.

What could I take with me?

What did I have to leave behind?

It was such a time of struggle and sadness, and yet there was excitement too.

What did the holy one of the mountain have in store for us?

Time would reveal my future.

After giving away, selling or throwing out most of my possessions, I took only what I needed: clothing, carpets, and items for meal preparation.

I first chose three things that were important to me. Things to connect me with my former life, and to help me to live in this new land we were going to.

I took my mixing bowl. It had been carved by my father for my mother. When I married she gave it to me and so this beautiful but very practical bowl was very special to me. It represented food and nourishment for us, for I mixed my bread in it, and prepared the grains for our meal. I made the same things that mother had and I received great comfort from making bread and lentils and stews in this wonderful bowl.

But it also represented my roots. As long as I had it, I could remember and feel connected to my past. My family. My history. My roots. When I washed it, I remembered that I was connected to a long line of people, stretching back for many years. People who had learned many lessons and had passed them on— life lessons, practical lessons and lessons about the God who spoke from the clouds. My mixing bowl was for nourishment and connection, both so necessary to life.

I also took my prayer mat. The mat I knelt on morning and night. Each morning I asked for guidance for the day, for patience, for understanding and for a sense of God's presence. Each evening I returned to it in gratitude for the day. Thankful for safety, for food, for family—for all those things that made my life a wonderful adventure. It was my reminder of God's presence and a source of strength and comfort. In times of loneliness or fear, that mat and my daily prayers, gave me strength and courage to face the difficult times. It was also the place where I sometimes stood with arms outstretched in thanksgiving for all the blessings in my life. And it was the place where I prayed each day for a son, the heir to Abraham and a sign of our commitment to each other, and of God's blessing.

And lastly, I took my little oil lamp. As I lit it each evening, it made me feel at home. It was the one I had used as a girl, and it was exactly like my mother's old, well-used lamp. It chased away the shadows in the tent and as it flickered, the colours of my rugs and my cloaks danced in the light of the flame. It was a small light, but it spread around the tent and made it feel like home. On chilly nights, by sitting close, I could feel the gentle warmth coming from that tiny flame. It lit the tent, it shone into my memories, and it warmed my heart.

But it had another deeper meaning. Our God was a God of fire. And so that little lamp was a reminder of God's eternal presence. We worshipped the God of the mountains where fire and smoke made the earth tremble with the power and the presence of God. El Shaddai, as we called our God, and to Abraham was God Almighty. Abraham related to God's power and might, and I understood that. But the name also meant the breasted one—a God who nurtures and sustains us. It was to that nurturing, mothering God I prayed my prayers: that the holy light of El Shaddai would nurture life in our people and in my womb and that I would bear a son.

How long must I wait?

Hear my prayers El Shaddai.

Hear my prayers and answer.

* * *

Questions for Contemplation or Discussion

1. What are Sarah's strengths?

2. How can she serve as an inspiration and a role model to modern women?

3. Is there a woman in your family who has been a role model for you? Share your story of a matriarch in your life.

Shiprah

Exodus 1:15-22

Background

In the years following the death of Joseph, the Israelites in Egypt begin to proliferate. The Egyptian king sought to curb the Israelite population lest its numbers threaten the security of Egypt in time of war. So Pharaoh commanded the Hebrew midwives, of whom only two are known by name—Shiphrah and Puah—to kill at birth all the male Hebrews, but to permit the females to live. However, because the midwives stood in awe of God, they violated Pharaoh's command and permitted the boys to live.

* * *

I remember those days very well. It seems but yesterday. We all lived in fear of the Pharaoh. To the Egyptians he was god. We Hebrews knew he was just a man, but a man with total power over us. We had been in Egypt for generations and the story of our going to that land of plenty was well known to all our people. Over the centuries, our numbers had grown. We were a strong race, and our dietary rules kept us healthy. Our babies and children thrived in spite of the harsh conditions.

Pharaoh was getting worried because he could see our numbers growing each year. While he was glad to have more slaves to work his brick pits and drag the stones for his tomb, he was aware that we were a people who longed for our freedom. He had heard talk of a deliverer who would come and lead us to freedom. Being a man of war, he could think of no other way for this to happen except by open warfare, and he decided to take steps to keep us in captivity.

He reasoned that if we had no young men, we could not go to war, and so he sent out a decree to the midwives that we were to kill Hebrew baby boys at birth. The girls could live. They would still be slaves and could work for him as we had done for many, many years.

I met with Puah and we talked and talked about what we could do. Mid-wives aid birth and they help to bring life; they do not destroy life. We knew we could not carry out this cruel, evil order. But what to do?

As women who worshipped the God of our foremothers, we knew that we had to find a solution. Our God was a God of life, and hope and promise, not a God of death and destruction.

Meeting with other mid-wives we talked for hours. We gathered in secret and whispered our fears, hopes and dreams. Many ideas were considered, some of them just foolish, but with openness and trust and the wisdom of women in community, at last we came up with the plan. We would disobey Pharaoh and the baby boys would live.

All of us were afraid. Pharaoh would soon know that the baby boys were not being killed at birth and we knew his anger would be upon us with the full force of his power. But we knew we had to save the precious babies.

Sure enough, in a very short time, Puah and I were called before Pharaoh. We were the head of the mid-wives and it was to us his orders came, and so we were called to answer for the fact of the living babies.

With fear and trembling in our hearts, we stood and tried our best to look confident and speak with authority. When asked why the babies lived we had our explanation ready and well-rehearsed. I told him that Hebrew women were strong and healthy, not like Egyptian women who were not as vigorous, and we couldn't get to them in time. When we were summoned, we went at once, but the Hebrew women had already given birth, and it was too late to snuff out that life at birth.

He believed our story and let us go. No doubt he would begin planning another tactic, but for now at least the babies were safe.

Time passed and I continued to do my work as mid-wife and I was blessed by God. I bore many children, sons and daughters, and I was happy to see them healthy and growing each year. But I still faced my life as a slave, as did all our people.

We lived as a people, faithful to the God of our ancestors and confident that the one who created the earth, gave his people a beautiful garden, and led us to food when we were starving, would hear our cries at last and send the deliverer to lead us to freedom.

I look forward to the day when my children live in freedom in their own land.

* * *

Questions for Contemplation or Discussion

1. How would you describe Shiprah?

2. There are a number of references in the Bible that suggest that God is a mid-wife to creation. Is this a new idea for you? How do you respond to this metaphor for God?

3. In what way has God been a mid-wife to you? What have you given birth to? Art, poetry, music, love, charity, kindness?

Tirzah

Numbers 26:33, 27:1-11, 36:1-13,
Joshua 17:3-6

Background

Zelophehad was a man who had no sons but five daughters. He died in the wilderness while the people were journeying to their new homeland. By law the daughters could not inherit and his five daughters went to Moses to plead their case for justice in the name of their father.

* * *

It all seems so very long ago and indeed it was. We were in the wilderness after our exodus from Egypt. We travelled for many years in the desert and there were hardships and challenges. We had expected many of these: the heat, the winds, the challenge of finding food and water, but others were unanticipated.

I had four sisters, and we were all the family my father had. I know that he wished he had sons but he loved us, and treated us with fairness and equality. He had treated our mother as a friend and partner, not a possession, and he raised us to be women who knew their worth and deserved fair treatment.

After mother died, we became his life. Our family travelled with the others and we were all hoping to build a new life for ourselves when we reached the land promised to us by our God. But it was not to be. Father died and we buried him in the desert. It was hard to leave him there, but we knew we would never forget him and what he had taught us.

He raised us to be wise, thoughtful and strong and we were used to equality. The law under which we lived stated that daughters could not inherit the family assets. At their marriage, daughters were given a dowry and it was thought that was sufficient security for women. The five of us agreed that we were the only heirs of our father and should inherit the land he would have been assigned in the new homeland. We decided to take our case to Moses.

He listened as we talked, frowning a lot, and fiddling with his beard. We felt that he was listening carefully, but was very much aware of the law and the criticism he would face if he acted outside of it. We had spoken to the other leaders and law-givers and we knew Moses had a difficult decision. He said that this was a very difficult matter and he needed time to think and to ask God for help in his decision.

In a few days he called everyone together: the priests, the elders and the congregation. He stated that we should be given the right to our father's lands. We were so very happy. It meant we would each have two shares in the new homeland to call our own. A place where we could live and raise our children, die and be buried with dignity.

But that wasn't the end. We were called back to the tent again and the case was to be re-considered. The elders stated that if we were to marry outside of our tribe, the land would go to our husbands and be lost to the tribe of Manasseh, our fathers tribe. There was much discussion and arguing and I finally spoke up and stated that we promised to marry within our tribe if we would be allowed to choose our own husbands. After the noise died down, and reason prevailed, it was agreed that we could choose our husbands from members of the tribe of Manasseh. It made sense to us, as we had no fathers or brothers to arrange our marriages.

When we came to the land across the river to which God led us, we were given our father's shares. In the next few years, we each married a member of our tribe.They were good marriages for we chose carefully. We could have married men who were simply interested in our land and would have treated us as slaves after they had taken possession of us and of our land. But we had been taught that we were of value, and we had lived with dignity and freedom, and were not prepared to become property of some ambitious, greedy land-grabber.

Over the years, we bore children, raised them in

the law, but also in the manner our father had raised us. Our sons were taught to respect women and to treat them fairly. Our daughters were taught respect for their elders, but also respect for themselves as children of God and worthy of being treated with justice.

Now as I come to the end of my years, I think back at the daring and courage we had. To stand up to the priest, the elders, Moses and all the people was an incredible act of hope. But that is how we were raised. We were taught that God was a God of justice and that God's people could always live in hope.

Five women, not much more than girls, changed the law for women for their betterment. We stood for what was right and we made a difference in the lives of women. Our parents did right by us and I am thankful.

* * *

Questions for Contemplation or Discussion

1. Think about these women and talk about them as role models.

2. How do you decide when a law is unjust and that it should be challenged?

3. How do we hold fast to our beliefs and practices while respecting the religion and culture of others?

Deborah

Judges 4:1-22: 5:1-31

Background

Deborah was a judge in Israel at the time of the judges. She lived in the hill country of Ephraim. Judges were not part of a legal system, but leaders, guides, councillors and prophets. She rode into battle against an invading army, giving leadership and courage during a time of war. She was a woman of great stature among her people.

* * *

There is nothing that I enjoy more than to sit under this tree in the shade. I come here so often the people are starting to call it Deborah's tree. These few minutes before the people gather give me a chance to reflect on all that has happened. Here I feel very close to the Holy One—the God who was worshipped by our foremothers in the days long past, and is still a very real presence in our lives today. I sit here and remember the stories our people tell of God's care and mercy.

We still tell the stories of our slavery in Egypt, of making bricks, day after day, week after week, and year after year. Generations of my people did not know freedom. Children were born, grew up and died in slavery, always afraid of the lash and the whip of the task masters. But God heard our cries and sent the deliverer, Moses. We marched out of Egypt into the wilderness. We endured thirst and hunger, hot winds and blowing sand that stung our faces. The children cried, the women wept, and the men talked of returning to Egypt and the slave pits.

Again our God heard our cries and provided for us by the hand of Moses. Water gushed from a rock for our thirsty throats, and manna appeared every morning to ease our hunger. At last, after many years, we crossed the river to our new homeland. Here we grow our dates and olives, grain and corn. Sheep and cattle graze on the hillside and in the meadows. Fish abound in our rivers and streams. Our children play happily in the streets and the women laugh and sing as they go to the well for fresh, cool water. Our cooking fires send wonderful aromas to the heavens and we thank God for our safety in this land.

But recently there arose a threat from the armies of Sisera. They saw our good and pleasant life and came with their swords and spears to take what God had given to us. Our general Barak, was a good and wise man, and when I summoned him he was ready to march against the invaders. He understood that our safety depended on God as much as it did on our weapons and our army and he knew that our people needed a symbol of God's help. He asked me to ride in the chariot with him, saying if I didn't he wouldn't go to battle. He recognized that our army needed a living symbol of the greatness of our God. After a dreadful battle, the enemy was defeated and returned to their land, and I returned to my seat beneath my tree.

And once again we live in peace and I can sit here and feel God's presence. Oh, I hear voices and the people are coming to talk with me. They share their struggles, their fears, their dreams and hopes. If there are quarrels, I help them to find a solution. If they are afraid, I remind them of our wonderful God. Some have a dream or a vision and I encourage them to find a way to make it come true for the good of our people.

God's people, if they seek wisdom and strength from the Holy One will live in peace.

May it always be so.

Thanks be to God.

* * *

Questions for Contemplation or Discussion

1. Deborah was known as a Mother in Israel. What characteristics do you think she had to merit this title?

2. How is her life an example for women today?

3. Are there women prophets in our time? Name some and talk about their voice in the world today.

Abigail
I Samuel 25:1-42
2 Samuel 3:3

Background

We know nothing of Abigail's family or of her early life. We can see from the text she was intelligent and quick to take action. Her action saved the lives of many people and her beauty and charm won David's heart. She may have been the only one of his eight wives and ten concubines that David married for love and not for political reasons.

* * *

When I think back on my life I am amazed. I can see now how good can come out of evil. When we are faithful to God and true to our faith and our nature, we can help ourselves and improve our lives. I didn't see all of this at the time, but my life shows me that God can be trusted if we are obedient to the commandments.

I was married to Nabal when I was very young. From the beginning I knew my life would be a difficult one. His favourite pastime was emptying his flask of wine. When he was drunk, which was most of the time, he was rude, mean, and often violent. He insulted our neighbours, our friends, and those he needed to do business with. I spent much of my time, trying to mend the relationships he had broken and I very quickly learned the skills of apologizing, negotiating, and appeasing angry women and men.   When he was drunk, Nabal knew no boundaries, had no sense of decency or polite, kind behaviour.

The work of the farm became my job to oversee and manage. Our workers would listen to him and nod and then come to me for their tasks. They knew he would never remember what he had told them to do, but he would take the credit for any job well done. As long as the task was done, and the farm prospered, I didn't mind.

Saul was our king, but he was weak and many said he was mad. David was living in the hills, waiting for his chance to take over the throne. Some said that he had been anointed by Samuel to be our king. I knew little about the politics of this, but did know about David and his band of warriors living and hiding in the nearby hills.

He sent a messenger to our farm, asking for food for his men. Nabal refused and sent the man away with curses and he even threw stones at him. When I heard of it, I was certain that we would be subject to David's wrath for he would not let this insult pass. Hospitality to a stranger was one of the rules by which we lived as a people of the Holy One.

Nabal went to his couch to sleep, and I knew he would be there for hours. I decided to try and save the situation. I gathered meat and cheese, bread, fruit and wine, and with a number of donkeys to carry my gifts, I set out to find David. It was my intent to make peace with him and to save our lives and our vineyards, cattle and fields, if I could.

When I found David, I fell at his feet. I told him that my husband was a man of bad character, and I reminded David that God was the one who gave life and took it away. I reminded David that vengeance belonged to God. I said that his enemies would be destroyed because of God's justice, and his own house would endure. I asked for mercy and also, that when God had fulfilled everything He had promised, that David would remember me with kindness.

David accepted my gifts and my words and he returned to the hills with provisions for his men. I returned to face Nabal. When he learned of what I had done, he realized how close he had been to bringing us to total disaster. He went to his bed and stayed there in a drunken stupor. I found him a few days later, dead.

Time has passed and my life is changing. David professed his admiration and respect for me, and we have learned to love each other. We are to be married in a few weeks. I cannot believe that I will be a wife to King David. I know there are others, but they are political wives, chosen for the good of the kingdom.

I am the one he truly loves and trusts.

May God bless our marriage with sons.

Blessed be the name of the Lord, who has done great things.

* * *

Questions for Contemplation or Discussion

1. In scripture there are references that state a wife should obey her husband. Was Abigail right or wrong in what she did? Why?

2. When you are in a crisis, how does your faith help you to deal with it?

3. Do you know women who have spoken words of wisdom in your life, or in our time?

Huldah

2 Kings 22:11-20,
2 Chronicles 34:22-28

Background:

Huldah is called a prophet for her role as a leader in her time. She lived at the same time as Jeremiah and Zephaniah. Because she had lived through the reign of three kings, she must have had a reputation for speaking for God and being loyal to him when the rest of society was abandoning him and putting their faith in other things. Hilkiah, the priest, knew her and came to her in a crisis.

* * *

I am a woman, one of my people, and yet rare among women here in Jerusalem. Shallum, my husband, was the keeper of the wardrobe in the temple. I worked beside him. We are partners in our work and in our lives. As the years passed, I have heard the holy words read and sung many, many times and I have learned them by heart and they have drawn me very close to the holy one. These words speak to me. Day and night as I ponder the stories of my people I see the hand of God in our lives. God nurturing us, teaching us, leading us, protecting us, calling us to new ways of being the people of God.

Our history was one of sorrow in our ancient times. We were in bondage in Egypt, slaves to the Pharaoh for generations until our liberation by Moses. Many, many years later our people were taken captive to Babylon and once again we wept—wept for our homeland, wept for our children, wept for all the lost ones and wept for our freedom. But thanks be to God we are once again home. We are rebuilding our homes and our shops, our streets, our walls and our sacred places.

The priests came to me one day, all dressed up in their finery, looking very serious and important. I wondered why they were seeking me, and I sensed some anxiety as they stood before me. I greeted them respectfully, and then waited for them to speak. They nudged one another, nodded back and forth and finally the old one spoke.

He told me of a scroll that they had found when clearing some rubble from the walls. An ancient scroll, dusty and dirty, ragged with age and abuse. But they knew that the words were important and King Josiah needed to know what they said. They asked for my interpretation.

I wondered why they did not consult Jeremiah or Zephaniah who were well known prophets in our country. But they came to me. Perhaps it was easy for them, since I lived nearby and they just walked to my home. However, it also might be that I was well known and respected as a prophet in our land. There was a group of followers of mine that wanted the two southern gates to the Temple Mount named the Huldah Gates. That is where I could be found praying and meditating, and it is where people came to hear God's message proclaimed as I spoke the wisdom which God revealed to me.

The people of my land were straying far from the commandments of the Holy One. There was evil in our land, and discontent and fear. I wondered if these men, in their robes of importance, were afraid to risk the anger of the king. Were they hiding behind a woman's skirts? It didn't matter. A prophet cannot be silent when there is God's word to be spoken. The message was clear and it was not a message of hope.

I spoke the words. "Thus says the Lord," the sign of a prophet, and I told them that we had forgotten our covenant with God, we had ignored our tithes and offerings, we profaned our holy places, and our prayers were just empty words, words, words. Our actions were the underlying building stones for our loss of hope and purpose as a people, and we were lax in our obedience to God.

The king took my words seriously. He decreed reforms, calling the people back to the ways of our forebears. But we had drifted too far away from God and evil times lay ahead. The days of tribulation were once more upon us.

But in my heart, I know that God is merciful and just. I don't know when or how, but we will find our way back to God. We will once again look to the hills where our courage and faith have always been found. The words of this old woman, and other prophets of God, will be the call to turn again to the one who is our Lord and our Shepherd.

* * *

Questions for Contemplation or Discussion

1. What kind of woman do you think Huldah was? How would you describe her?

2. Why do you think Jeremiah and Zephania have a book included in the Hebrew scriptures and there is not a book named after Huldah? Was it just because she was a woman, or is there more to it? What other reasons can you think of?

3. When have you been given good advice you didn't want to hear? How did you respond?

Chapter 2
Mothers, Wives and Queens

Listen to Their Stories

Women fill many roles in their lives and in the Bible they are most often identified by a male with whom they have a relationship. Three common motifs in Biblical material are Mothers, Wives, and Queens.

This count is not complete but I very easily found in an index in the book, *Woman Witness* by Miriam Therese Winters ©1992 by The Crossroad Publishing Company which cited: twenty wives, twenty-eight daughters, twelve mothers, four widows and two sisters, none of whom were named. The Queens, interestingly, were nearly always named and there were eleven in this source. Only the Queen of Sheba has no reference to a male relative or King in her realm.

These women all had a wonderful story that needed to be told. Their influence and impact on the nation and its history merited recording their role, even in those patriarchal times. Whether they were a mother, a wife or a Queen, their contribution was noted as an important part of the story

Some of their names are noted in the Bible, others are found in Jewish writings, but the name of the wife of Lot is my choice. As I stated in the introduction I have chosen to name the unnamed as a way to honour their contribution to the story and their place in it.

Many of these women have been depicted by great artists over the years and it is an interesting journey to find the paintings, and study the way in which the woman is depicted. Many can be found at sites on the internet.

Hazelelponi
Mother of Samson
Judges 13:2-25; 14:1-9; 16: 30-31

Background:

Samson was dedicated as a Nazarite at his birth. It meant a vow to abstain from alcohol and to never cut one's hair. His mother lived that consecrated life during her pregnancy. She was a woman who trusted in her God. This name is given to her in Jewish writings.

* * *

As an ordinary woman, I expected an ordinary life. And it was. My only sorrow was my barren, empty womb. I longed for a son as did every woman in my time. It was the one thing that validated us and gave our lives meaning.

One day was anything but ordinary. A messenger came to me and told me that I would bear a son. The messenger told me that I was to live as a Nazarite and my son was to be given to God on the day of his birth. He too was to be raised as a Nazarite. Then I was told that he had been chosen by God to begin the delivery of Israel from the oppression of the Philistines.

I told my husband, Manoah, and I could see he was trying hard to understand. He prayed to his God and asked to be taught what to do with the boy. The angel came again to me, and I took this messenger to Manoah so that he could see and hear and learn. He re-told us all that he had told me. We offered to make a meal for our guest, but we were told to offer a burnt offering to God.

We prepared the lamb from our flock and grain from our fields. The fire was lit, and the messenger disappeared in the smoke. We fell to the ground and worshipped this holy One.

The time passed quickly and my son was born. He came into the world howling and screaming. And that is the child that I was trying to raise to be God fearing, gentle and wise. He grew strong and proud, and we were blessed by God. His hair was never cut, and his strength was more than that of an ordinary man.

He was good to us, his parents, but he had a quick temper and he was very disturbed by the Philistines. I knew that he was destined to free us from their yolk, but his anger and rage alarmed me.

He went about the country and I heard rumours about his deeds. It was said that he killed a lion with his bare hands. Later he found a hive of bees in the carcass of the lion and took some honey as he walked along the road. I had to believe this story when I heard it, for he came home one day and gave us a great amount of honey.

His father could not refuse him anything he asked for, as he feared Samson's anger. This only fuelled his need to be obeyed. When he asked Manoah to make marriage arrangements with a woman of the Philistines, I was very disturbed.

What would become of his vow as a Nazarite? What good could come of marrying into the people he despised?

It all turned out badly. The woman was only the first of a number of women that helped to bring about my son's downfall. We heard frightening stories of his skirmishes with the enemy, and I was afraid that my son was lost to me and to our God.

One woman cut off his hair, breaking his Nazarite vow, his strength was gone and he was captured by the Philistines. While in captivity his hair grew long again and his strength returned. In the end he pulled down a house and killed everyone who was there—everyone, including himself.

I claimed his body and brought him home and buried him beside his father. I had done my best, but Samson was a great disappointment. I wonder if God has been as disappointed in him as I was? Or was it all part of God's plan.

I wonder, and will wonder about it until the day I die.

* * *

Questions for Contemplation or Discussion

1.   There are many stories of barren women who gave birth to a special child. How does this story differ from any others you have read?

2.   Do you think that this kind of destruction is ever the will of God? Why or why not?

3.   How does a mother deal with a child who does not live up to their potential?

Abijah
Mother of Hezekiah
II kings 18:1-5
II Chronicles 29: 1

Background

Abijah, often called Abi, was the wife of King Ahaz, and the mother of King Hezekiah. King Ahaz was a ruler in a long line of Judah's kings who were weak and corrupt, however, their son, King Hezekiah, was described as being a man of God and there was none like him in the history of Judah.

* * *

I lie here on my bed, and it is to be my death bed. I know that I have little time left. My husband Ahaz has long ago gone to sleep with his fathers. Married very young, we had a chance to do much good and to re-shape the life of the people of Judah. But Ahaz could not be the man the kingdom needed. He was a weak and idolatrous man. My grief was deep and my pain unforgivable when he offered our son to the flames of the pagan god Moleck. He tried to buy the loyalty of foreign rulers, even to making a copy of one of their idols and bringing it back and placing it in the temple. But it was all a failure, as he was.

A queen must always show public loyalty to her royal husband and master, but it was all a show. I did not hate him, for hate is destructive to the one who holds on to it, but I had no respect for him, no admiration or fidelity to his kingship. We had no affection for each other. He was king and I was a prized possession. It was my duty to provide him with sons, and I did.

My son, Hezekiah was my joy and my delight. He was a wonderful baby: happy, contented, strong and healthy. I made a vow to the Holy One that I would raise this child to be a God fearing man—a man of justice, compassion and wisdom. He would be a ruler who would make Judah great again. As a daughter of the High Priest Zechariah, I knew what was needed in a leader, and I had the faith and the knowledge to train him to be a good king.

I surrounded him with servants who were also followers of the Holy One who would teach him the ways of our ancestors. He was told the stories of Abraham, Moses, Joshua and David. As he grew he was schooled in numbers, language, history and proper court procedures. A very bright and clever boy, he learned quickly and understood that he was to be the king one day. At every opportunity, I taught him that idol worship, the desecration of the temple and the evil he saw around him was going to be the downfall of the kingdom. When he became king, I said it would be his

42

task to bring the nation back to God and to reform life in every way for the people.

I did not keep him from his father, but never left him alone with him, and kept his visits brief and when Ahaz was in a pleasant mood. At times I lied and said the boy was not well when I suspected that Ahaz had something unwholesome in his mind and plans.

When Ahaz died, he was so disliked that he was not buried with the kings, and on the day of his death, the sun shone for only two hours. It was as if even the heavens were darkened by his life.

Hezekiah was only twenty-five when he came to the throne. But he was ready. He defeated the armies of Sennacherib and made the land safe once again. With foreign invasion no longer a threat he could restore the kingdom.

He has begun many reforms. The temple has been cleansed of all the abominations that had become a part of the building and the rituals. The Passover pilgrimage to Jerusalem has been restored and the people once more remember our liberation from slavery and offer thanksgiving. All the idols in the high places are being destroyed and the people will look to the hills to find the God of our ancient people as they did in the past.

I have spent my life preparing my son for this task. He is a good and just king, trusting in the God of Israel. I will not live to see the nation restored to its former greatness, or all the people once again worshipping the God of the mountains and the plains. But I can rest knowing that I did what was right and I did what God needed me to do. My life has not been in vain.

If I am remembered at all, I will be happy to be remembered as the mother of the good and righteous King Hezekiah.

* * *

Questions for Contemplation or Discussion

1. In this chapter there are eight women named as the mothers of kings. There are four others listed as mothers of kings, but unnamed. Why was it important to make a note of these women?

2. Women in this time had very little power. Even most queens were confined to the duties of wife and mother. What do you know of the role of Jewish mothers in the home regarding religious duties?

3. What role did your mother, or another woman, play in your spiritual life? Is the role of a mother important today for the family's spiritual life and understanding?

Machla

Meaning ornament
Wife of Lot
Genesis 19: 1-26

Background

We remember the story of Lot's wife being turned into a pillar of salt because she looked back as she left the city of Sodom. We know nothing about her before this story. Lot's marriage is never mentioned. Since he had gone to Sodom to live, it is likely that his wife was from this city.

* * *

He came to our city to live. A man of the desert. He strode into my life: wealthy, strong and very sure of himself. We married and settled into our lives in the city of my birth. My family accepted him, mostly I think, because of his riches and his lively manner.

Lot spoke sometimes of his uncle Abraham and I knew they had separated under a cloud of disagreement. But it never seemed to bother him very much that his only family was my family. Whatever his life had been before, he became one of us in many ways, but he still paid homage to the God of his life before he arrived in Sodom. We spoke of this God at times, and I found this God of my husband interesting and somewhat appealing. Lot also talked to our daughters and taught them the ways of his people. I had no objection, for to me, one god is as good as another.

Sodom was a wild city. There were things that happened that we did not speak of in our home. Lot just said it was unspeakable and we talked of other things. But he was critical of the way the people were only interested in their own well-being. There was no thought for the stranger in our midst. There was little charity for the poor. Beggars were ignored or given a kick or a shove to get them out of the way. Hospitality for the stranger did not exist.

I knew that the only reason Lot was allowed to settle and be a part of our world, was that he came with great riches. He had flocks of geese, and many cattle and sheep. His donkeys were the finest I had ever seen, and there were many bags that looked as if they held money or other valuable goods. This was why he was accepted, and this was why I was given to him in marriage.

I remember our last night in the city very well. It was a night of great noise with shouting and cursing. Two strangers had come to our house, and Lot told me and our daughters to hide in the back and be very quiet. I had no idea what happened, but I heard people hammering on the door trying to get in.

After a long time, things got quiet and we slept on the floor wrapped in our cloaks, still hiding. In the morning Lot came and said we were leaving. He said his God was angry and the city was going to be destroyed. He said we had to leave at once and there was no time to take any of our possessions.

This strange and angry God had agreed that we could go and live in the nearby town of Zoar. I knew nothing about it and I didn't want to leave the place of my birth. I had grown up in this city; it was all I knew. My parents were buried here, as were my babies who had died. My family, my aunts and uncles were here, friends from my youth and childhood, all the memories of my life. And now I was expected to leave this because some God said, "Go." It didn't make sense, but he was my husband and we had to obey him.

Lot said the city was to be destroyed by fire, and everyone would die. We were to leave at once and not look back. Our daughters were told by Lot to get moving and then he ordered me to follow him. And so we left everything behind. Once again he said, "Remember, do not look back."

We set out and were climbing the hill travelling very quickly to get out of town, heading in the direction of Zoar. At the top of the hill, as we were about to start our descent, I turned my head . . .

* * *

Questions for Contemplation of Discussion

1. What do you feel toward Lot's wife? Judgement? Pity? Compassion? Derision? Blame? Understanding?

2. Is it wrong to look back on our lives? What can be gained?

3. Jesus said that we are to be the salt of the earth? What does it mean to be like salt?

Queen Vashti

Esther 1: 1-21

Background

At a royal banquet, such as this one, the wife of the king would not be present, only his concubines. The queen was kept secluded from the excesses of such a scene of debauchery. Scripture says she was summoned to come wearing her crown. Some interpret this to mean that she was naked, except for the crown. This cannot be proved and it does not matter. Queen Vashti had self-worth and dignity and due to her refusal, was banished.

* * *

Here I am. A queen no more. Now a daughter once again living in her father's household. It is fine with me. I was born a Persian princess and I will die a Persian princess. What a twist my life has taken.

My marriage to King Ahasuerus was a magnificent wedding. No expense was spared, and the feasting went on for days. I was impressed with his show of power and riches, and now I was the queen in this vast kingdom. I didn't need all the pomp and splendour, but it pleased my new husband and so I relaxed and enjoyed the many days of celebration.

49

Life was much as I had expected: rich food, servants, wonderful rooms in which to live, and women to keep me company and care for my every need. While I enjoyed it, I didn't let it become important to me. My belief was that virtue and dignity were the garments that should be worn by a queen. Truth and honour, the crown for my head, and concern for the people of our land, my cloak and mantle.

The king gave a royal banquet for all his officials and officers. I knew it would last for days, and so decided to give a banquet one evening for the women of the palace. It was fun to dress up in our finest and have a lovely meal together without having to worry about what the king would do, or say, or think.

Ahasuerus paraded all his wealth before the men: his horses and chariots, his jewels and fine robes, his most opulent crown. He had the room prepared with gold and silver couches, fine linen hangings, marble and mother-of-pearl floors, and golden goblets for everyone. On the last day, I could hear the drunken singing, laughter and shouting even in my rooms. I was glad that it would soon be over and things could return to normal.

Just as I was thinking of retiring for the night seven eunuchs came to my door. They said the king wanted me to come to him so that his guests might look upon his beautiful wife. I was shocked. A queen is kept in seclusion. Men do not gaze upon her. Even the wives of ordinary people lead quiet dignified lives in the company of only the males in their families. I could not believe this, and I dismissed the eunuchs. They at once demanded I listen to them. The king ordered me to appear before him so he could show his guests his most prized possession.

My face became red with anger and with shame. I was a queen, a person, a woman of dignity and worth. I was respectable and knew my self-worth as a woman who was also a queen. I would not go before his drunken friends to be made an object of their drunken lust.

I refused, and shut and barred the door.

The next morning I was awake early and waited for the consequences of my behaviour. I knew that the king would have been humiliated with my refusal. I knew that I would pay a great price for what I had done. But I had no regrets. The news came soon. I was to be banished from the kingdom.

And so I am back at my parent's home. And I hear that the king is holding a beauty contest for my replacement. Whoever she is I hope she is strong, wise, brave and a woman of character and uprightness. I wish her well, and may her gods protect her.

* * *

Questions for Contemplation and Discussion.

1. How do you respond to the refusal of Vashti?

2. In what ways does the understanding that women must obey their husbands, and that a man should be the master in his own house, affect women today?

3. Have you ever defied male authority and, if so, what was the result?

Nitzevet
Mother of David
I Samuel 22: 3-4

Background

These two verses are the only mention in scripture of David's mother. Her name is not recorded. Some Jewish writings give her the above name. Jesse, her husband, had eight sons and two daughters. With no mother named, we assume that they were all born of the same mother.

* * *

He was my youngest child, my baby, the child of my later years. He was named David which means beloved, and I loved him dearly, but as the youngest he was always given the worst of the jobs that had to be done. Shepherds are not liked in our land; they smell of sheep, and lead rough, crude and dangerous lives. It pained me to see my beloved son David treated this way, but I could do nothing. I made sure he was well fed, always sending food with him. I taught him how to treat wounds, scratches from brambles and thorns, and treat cuts and bruises. I hoped and prayed he would not have any serious injuries.

53

Being a shepherd was a difficult and lonely task. It was his job to fight off wild animals and robbers who came after our sheep. He had to protect the animals as they fed, wandering from plant to plant oblivious to danger. I insisted that Jesse teach him how to use his staff and his rod—the staff to rescue and carry the sheep, the rod to ward off snakes and predators. He also taught him to use a sling and David became very skilled in the use of that weapon. These simple skills were all that I, his mother, could do to protect him. No harm came to him and I was grateful for his safety.

One day there was great excitement. The prophet Samuel came to visit. He asked to see all our sons, as he had been told by God to anoint the chosen one to be the next king after Saul. The seven eldest all went before him, and he did not choose any one of them. Jesse came to get David, but I could tell he thought it foolish. But I had a very good feeling about this. Somehow a mother sees in her children what others cannot.

Samuel recognized David as the one, and he was anointed with oil. I knew then that our lives had changed forever.

My son was a wonderful musician and poet and Saul called David to play his harp for him and to sing to him. The day came when there was a battle with the army of the Philistines. Imagine it! Against their champion, a giant called Goliath, all the great armies of Saul were useless—yet my son killed him with his slingshot. I am glad I only knew about that after it was all over. But Saul was getting uneasy about David. He knew that David was becoming very popular amongst the people. Someone had foolishly told him that while he, Saul, had killed a thousand, David had killed ten thousand. And in his madness Saul tried to kill him.

David had to hide from Saul's rage and anger. He was also afraid for our safety, and took us into the land of Moab to the palace of the king. Our ancestor Ruth was from the land of Moab, and so there were some connections there. David returned to the land of Israel to wait for the prophecy of Samuel to be fulfilled.

We heard many things about David after he became king. He was a great warrior, who subdued many enemies, including the Philistines. He united our divided kingdom and brought the Ark of the Covenant to Jerusalem. He had plans to make that beautiful city, set on a hill, the political, cultural and religious centre of our land. David had eight wives and many concubines.

He is a great king, and I knew that greatness lived in my young son. He will make mistakes for he is proud and headstrong, but he will be a king to be remembered. I pray every day for him and for his reign.

He is my son and he is heir to the promises of God. Our people will become a great and powerful nation under David's rule. A mother knows these things.

* * *

Questions for Contemplation or Discussion

1. The story of David's mother has been lost. If you were writing her story what would you add to this one?

2. What are some qualities and values that David might have learned from his mother?

3. What has your mother handed on to you? How will you keep her story and your story alive for future generations?

Jochebed

Mother of Moses

Exodus 2:1-10; 6: 20
Numbers 26: 59

Background

Jochebed was born into slavery. Both she and her husband were of priestly tradition by birth. They had two children: Miriam, about ten, and Aaron, three. When the mid-wives circumvented the edict of Pharaoh to kill the babies at birth, a new plan was decreed. All boy babies were to be drowned in the Nile River. It was at this terrible time that Jochebed gave birth to another son, Moses.

* * *

I lay here on my death bed. I may have a few hours or a few days, but the time is near for me to join my ancestors. There is no pain, only a deep sadness that I do not know what became of my third child.

He was destined to die by Pharaoh's decree, but he was such a beautiful baby that I had to fight for his life. What mother wouldn't? I managed to keep him hidden for a few weeks, but it became impossible. He had a good strong voice and when he cried I feared someone would hear him. I carried him with me at all times, suckling him whenever he stirred. But even his contented gurgles were becoming loud and now he was starting to laugh. I had to find another solution.

Watching the fishing boats going up and down the Nile gave me an idea. We made a little boat for him, and I placed him in it, and then carried him to the river. Gently I put the craft into the water, and through my tears watched it float near the shore where it was not going to get carried away by the swifter waters. Miriam stayed nearby and watched. She had courage, that daughter of mine. She waded into the water, not showing any fear of snakes or crocodiles.

The daughter of Pharaoh came to bath in the sacred waters with all her maids. She saw the basket and walked toward it. She lifted the lid, and saw the infant. He began to cry and she picked him up and began to sing to him. Miriam moved out of the shadows, and told the princess that she could find a woman to nurse him if she wished.

Just as we planned, she came and got me. Pharaoh's daughter agreed that I take this child home, care for him until he was weaned, and then bring him to her at the palace. I hugged him close to me and we went back to our simple home. She named him Moses, because she drew him out of the water.

When he was weaned—and I nursed him for longer than was common—I took him to the palace. In those years I had tried to teach him by the way he was treated, that kindness and gentleness, patience and love, were the way people should live. As I left him in that grand house of Pharaoh, I wondered if he would remember what I had tried to teach him.

For the second time in his short life, I left my child, and walked away from him.

The years passed, and we heard nothing about him. Then one day, my son Aaron came home and said that someone had killed an overseer who was whipping a Hebrew slave. No one could believe it, but it was the son of the princess and he had been banished to the desert.

My son, now a man, banished to the terrible wilderness. How can he live in that God forsaken place? But it is not God forsaken. The Holy One will be with him. I had to believe that.

And now as I lie here drawing my last breath, they tell me Moses has returned. He has come to free our people. I have lived to see my son, God's agent of deliverance, and now I can die in peace.

* * *

Questions for Contemplation or Discussion

1. Jochebed took an enormous risk. She trusted the daughter of the man who would kill her baby. What gave her the wisdom to think of this plan and the courage to follow through with it?

2. How much influence do you think those few early years of his childhood had on him as an adult?

3. Can you think of a woman who was as courageous as Jochebed? What did she do? Where did she get her courage and strength?

Chapter 3
Nameless Women

Women of Hope

The women in this chapter are not named in the Bible stories in which they are featured, however, each of them plays an important role in the developing story of God and the people who are God's followers.

Four of them are from the Hebrew Scriptures and two from the Christian Scriptures. Tova, the Samaritan woman, and Shaler, in the story of the feeding of the 5000, are from stories in the New Testament. Shaler is not present in the Biblical narrative at all, however, the young boy with the lunch in the story must have had a mother, and it is through her eyes I tell the story, as I imagine she lived it.

While these women, the pivotal centre of the narratives, are not named, their stories are rich and powerful. Miracles swirl around these women. Miracles of healing, miracles of nurturing with food and with knowledge, and miracles surrounding the freedom and birth of a nation.

Their roles are pivotal and the males in the stories could be seen to be in supporting roles. Since tradition was still in force, these women of courage and action were nameless.

In spite of this, their actions dominated the stories and instigated the changes that happened in people's lives. At times, this changed the history of the Hebrew people and greatly influenced the future of religion.

Bithia
Daughter of Pharaoh
Exodus 2:1-10

Background

If you have seen the movie about Moses' early life, you will remember that in it his mother was named Bithia. She is not named in the Bible story but this is the name that the Jewish Midrash gives to the Egyptian princess. Who she was has been lost in the passage of time, as has the identity of the Pharaoh.

* * *

I am the daughter of the Pharaoh. I am a princess of a great line of Egyptian rulers. Everything I desire I have: jewels, clothes, servants, slaves—the best that this country has to offer. Pharoah has not yet given me in marriage to anyone. Someday I know there will be a prince for me, but I am in no hurry to change my life as I have some independence. My father is too busy building temples and tombs to bother with me. I amuse myself as I choose. I should be happy but I am not. In spite of all the people constantly around me, I am lonely. There is no purpose to my life other than to be beautiful and obedient.

The suffering of the Hebrew slaves causes me great pain. They are human beings, not cattle, but they are treated as beasts of burden. I cannot watch their suffering; it makes me ill just to hear their cries for deliverance. It is said that they await a deliverer, but who can break the power of the Pharaoh?

My happiest times are when I go to the Nile to bathe. There is a quiet pool that is safe from crocodiles as it has a wall built to enclose it. The water is cool and clear and the surface is covered with beautiful lotus flowers. They are white, red, pink and blue and so there is always one to match the colour of my gown. I like to wear them in my hair, as their perfume is lovely.

One morning, a long time ago, a small woven basket floated into the pool. My maids brought it to me, and in it was a beautiful child, about three months old. I swore all my women to secrecy on pain of death if they told.

I knew at once that he was one of the Hebrew babies my father had ordered put to death. I looked around and a young woman was there, watching over him. I could see that she too was Hebrew and I called her to explain. She simply said, "I can find a wet nurse for him if you need one." I sent her away and told her to bring the woman to the palace.

When I showed her the baby, her face became a mirror of love and I knew she was his mother. I told her she could nurse the child and look after him until he was weaned. Since she had risked her life to save this child, I knew she would not give away his identity and she would care for him with all the love and tenderness of any mother for her child.

I named the baby Moses and grew to love him as my own son. When he was weaned, I decided to keep his mother for a while longer. I really had little patience with a young child and could wait until he was older to begin to school him in the ways of an Egyptian prince.

Too late I realized his mother was teaching him his own history. She taught him of their God and told him the stories of his people, so I sent her away and began to make him mine.

He learned the ways of our gods, he wore the locks of a prince of Egypt and he learned to write, to drive a chariot and wield a sword and shield. He was a tall handsome man and I began to think of him as Egyptian and my son, a Prince of Egypt.

But he never forgot what his mother taught him and he had the compassion that was my inner nature. He rose up against one of the taskmasters of the Hebrew slaves and killed him. My baby, my son Moses, has been banished to the desert. They gave him a little food and a wooden staff, mocking him as a prince of the desert.

From my window I watched him stride out across the sand until he was just a dot against the sky.

What a pharaoh he would have been. But he is gone. Gone from my life. Gone from my world. Gone from history.

* * *

Questions for Contemplation or Discussion

1. What characteristics would you ascribe to Bithia from the story?

2. Is one ever justified to disobey a law? Under what circumstances?

3. Do you know of a woman in later history who has done such a courageous thing? Share what you know about her.

Nessa

Shunammite Woman

Her name means miracle

2 Kings 4: 8-37

Background

According to the Biblical text she lived in Shumen and was a wealthy woman. She was a kind woman who offered help to a stranger, Elisha, a prophet. As the story opens she was childless and the text says her husband was old.

* * *

I would see him walking by on the road. He was covered in the dust of his travels, and I could tell that he was tired, hungry and thirsty. I invited him to stay with us and offered him a meal and a cool drink. He accepted, and whenever he passed by he always came to my home for rest.

After many such visits, I had my husband erect a small room for him on the roof of our home. We put a bed, a table and chairs and a lamp in it. It gave him a comfortable place to stay and sleep. We would talk late into the evening. The most wonderful stories of places he had been and seen, entertained us late into the day.

But he also talked to us about the Holy One and his message was one of peace and hope.

The neighbours said I was asking for trouble. They asked me what I knew of him and I said he was a man of God and that was all I needed to know. He was kind and gentle and very grateful for the simple things we did for him. Some warned me that I could find myself murdered in my bed, or he would burn the house down as he kept his lamp burning late into the night. But I was not afraid and continued to offer him our friendship.

One day he asked what he might do for me to repay my kindness. I replied that I needed nothing. But he knew. He knew that I longed for a son. And that day as he was leaving, he promised that a child would be born to us. I chided him for offering me false hope. But it wasn't long until I knew his words to be true.

What a joy and delight our son was. How wonderful to watch him grow; to hear his laughter and to listen for his footsteps when he was at home. He was a good boy and often went to the fields with his father. One day they carried him home and he said, "Mother, my head hurts." I held him in my arms, and tried to sooth his restlessness, and to give him my strength. But soon I knew he was gone. I could not imagine my life without him.

Gently I carried him up to the roof top room and laid him on the bed. My heart was broken but I knew what I must do. I called a servant, and he got our donkey ready and I rode as fast as I could to find Elisha. I found him at the mountain and fell at his feet. As soon as he heard, Elisha tried to send his servant, Gehazi to tend the boy, but I insisted that Elisha come home with me, and he did.

He went to the roof top, and entered the room shutting the door. I could hear him praying, and then pacing up and down in the room. I don't know what he did besides pray and pace. But in a little while—it seemed like a very long time—he came to me and said, "go to your son, he will be fine." And he was. Within a very short time, he was running and playing, laughing and singing once again. He followed his father to the fields and I worried each day until he came safely home. But he always did, talking about all he had seen and done as he learned the ways of a farmer from his father.

Such a blessing it is to have his voice filling our home with joy and laughter once again. It will be wonderful to watch him grow to be a man. Soon we will go to the temple for his blessing and he will be recognized as a son of the covenant and will join the men for discussion and prayer.

All this, because I gave a wandering prophet a place to rest and some bread and cheese. I expected nothing in return and I have been given the greatest gift of all. A son. Thanks be to the Holy One. Blessed is his name.

* * *

Questions for Contemplation or Discussion

1. How do you suppose Nessa knew that he was a holy man?

2. What did it mean for a woman to be childless in that time?

3. Do miracles still happen in our world? What can you name as miraculous in your life?

Tova
Meaning good
Samaritan Woman
John 4: 1-42

Background

This story took place in Samaria. Jews and Samaritans were not friendly towards each other; they might be considered enemies. Jesus stopped at the well to rest and get a drink. The woman who arrived should be despised by Jesus, a Jew. She was female, a Samaritan, and lived a questionable life style. However, he engaged in a long conversation with her.

* * *

As I always did, I went to the well for my water at noon. Not because I enjoyed doing such heavy work in the heat of the sun, but because I wanted to avoid everyone. The well is a gathering place for the women. They share their lives with each other, rejoice with one another and offer comfort in times of sadness or trouble. When I went and they were there, it often became totally silent. They stood back and let me get my water and then waited until I was almost out of earshot before they began to say the disparaging remarks I always heard. So it was more comfortable to go when I would be alone.

As I came over the hill I saw a figure sitting by the well. I decided that since I needed water I would just have to get it and leave as quickly as I could. As I drew closer I could see that it was a man sitting there. I stopped. Then went on. I didn't know if this would be better or worse, but I had no choice.

As I got closer I could see that he was a Jew. I wondered what he was doing in Samaria, but breathed a sigh of relief as I knew he wouldn't speak to me, so I was at least not going to face ridicule or abuse.

As I started to fill my water jars, the unbelievable happened. He asked me for a drink. Jews don't speak to any woman in public and certainly not to a foreigner in such a public place. But he wanted a drink. I challenged him that he had no cup and I was sure he would never share mine. We started to talk and he spoke of living water that satisfied and became a living spring of water dwelling inside.

Then he asked about my husband. I told him I had no husband. Somehow he knew. Knew that five men had rejected me because I was childless. I was married, then thrown aside. The man who was providing for me now did not marry me. Just took me in to cook, sew and clean for him. But there was no judgement in this man by the well in his voice or in his look. Just a gentle smile. I knew at that moment that this was a prophet, a man of God.

The conversation continued about where we should worship, and how we should worship God. We Jews and Samaritans had very different understandings and that is why we were so fearful of each other. We talked for a long time and I finally understood.

He said that God didn't really care where or how we worshipped. All our posturings, rituals and outward show didn't matter. God cared about what was in our hearts. He said, "God is spirit, and we need to worship in Spirit and in truth."

As the light of his truth dawned on me, I felt forgiven, understood and loved. I had to share this good news. I ran to the village, leaving my valuable water jar behind, and told everyone I met. They listened and then came to the well to hear for themselves.

On this trip to the well, I received more than fresh, cold water. I received a blessing from God and a whole new way to live. Thanks be to God.

* * *

Questions for Contemplation or Discussion

1. Where do you think the courage came from that enabled her to go to the village to share what she had learned?

2. What does it mean to you to worship in spirit and in truth?

3. There are many biblical stories about leaving things behind. Sarah left her home, the disciples left their nets, the shepherd left his sheep, and this woman left her water jar. What significance does this pattern of leaving have for you? What have you left behind in your life? How was God present in that event?

Azaryyah
Meaning God helps
Syrophoenician Woman
Mark 7: 24-30

Background

This woman was a Gentile, a Greek by birth from the area called Tyre and Sidon. By religion she would have been a Canaanite, a pagan, a foreigner and for this she was despised. She is persistent on behalf of her suffering child.

* * *

My beloved daughter was just a child when she became ill. They said she was possessed by a devil. I didn't know what was wrong but she was not a healthy child. Some days she would be sunny and happy, almost giddy and silly with her joy. Other days she was sad, very, very sad and she would cry most of the day. It is heartbreaking to watch your daughter sit in a corner and silently weep, hour after hour. There was nothing I could do that calmed her on her wild days, or cheer her when she was crying.

I had tried everything and was at my wits end. She was getting older, and I could not keep her condition secret. Many times people who suffered as she did were chained in an outlying place, often a grave yard. The thought of that made me desperate. I had to do something.

One day I heard about a Jew who was a healer. They called him Jesus, and he and his followers had done wonderful things in this area. I wondered how I could reach him, and then I heard he was near our village. Fortunately, my daughter was in one of her near normal stages, and I left her with my sister and went to seek this man, Jesus.

It was easy to find him. I simply followed the crowds. Gradually, I worked my way close to him and threw myself at his feet. I cried out my pain and begged for him to help me. He ignored me. He went on talking to people, laying hands on some of them, praying with them, and just stepping around me. I got to my feet, moved in front of him and knelt right in his way. He couldn't go around me, as the crowd was pressing in all around him.

Finally he looked down and turned his attention on me. I told him about my daughter and begged him to heal her. His followers tried to send me away, but I ignored them, and continued to plead with Jesus. Those around him told Jesus to give me what I wanted, mostly to get rid of me.

The words he spoke were like a slap in the face. He called me a dog. A dog! That is the worst insult a

Jew can throw at anyone. I didn't expect that. I had heard he was a gentle, kind healer. But I would take any insult he could give me. For my child I would bear anything.

I stood and looked up at him face to face. I would not crawl like the dog he called me. I lifted my chin and replied, "You say that you are not here for the likes of me. You say that the bread, your healing hand, is not meant for the likes of me. It is not for dogs of my kind." And then I reminded him that dogs eat the crumbs from the table of their masters.

He took a step backward and looked stunned. After a silent moment, a thoughtful look came over his face and I wondered what was going to happen to me.

I, a foreigner and a mere woman, had argued with a man, a Jew, a famous beloved Rabbi. I knew I had taken a terrible risk, but my daughter was what was important. Not my dignity, not my safety, not even my life, if there was a chance to help her.

He turned back to me and I looked into the kindest eyes that matched his gentle smile. Quietly he spoke. "Great is your faith, go home, it is done. All that you need has been accomplished."

I thanked him with a smile and a bow, and I hoped he knew how grateful I was. Then as fast as I could I went to my daughter.

She was indeed well. She met me with a hug and a smile. Not a wild laugh, not with deep felt tears, but a welcoming smile. She reached out to me and we hugged there in her room. The God of the Jews is indeed a gracious God who opened his arms to me an outcast and an outsider. I shall never forget his goodness. I will learn more of this rabbi and his teachings, and my daughter will know how she was healed.

* * *

Questions for Contemplation or Discussion

1. Reflect on the mother child bond and the extent a woman will go to protect her child. Do you have a story to share that illustrates deep motherly love?

2. Suppose this story had a different interpretation. Suppose it was the case of a strong-willed mother and a clever and determined young woman. If Jesus helped the woman to change her behaviour, it would change the circle of mistrust and anger. How do you feel about this interpretation of the story?

3. What torments and troubles young women today?

Shaler

Meaning Hope

Luke 9: 10-17

Background

This story is told in all four gospels, with minor differences in each. Apart from the resurrection of Jesus it is the only story told in all the gospels. Andrew is only named in John's Gospel, so the information used here is gathered from all the Gospel stories.

* * *

My name is Shaler and I live near the town of Bethsaida, a lovely fishing village which has been my home all my life. It is a prosperous village and the figs, dates, corn, and sheep that we grow and raise here on our farm find a ready market in the village.

I remember that day so very well. It began as an ordinary day, except that my son Obadiah did not have to go the rabbinic school. We called him Obi as his given name seemed so formal for such a happy child. The rabbi was sick and so the boys had a day to spend as they chose. Obi wanted to go the water for a day of fun. Some of his friends said they were going too.

He is not a little boy anymore and sometimes it is hard for me to remember that next year he becomes a man according to our custom. He will become one of the members of a minyan and begin studying Torah, but he will always be my little boy.

I got busy and packed him a small lunch. I had a few barley cakes and a couple of little fish. I wrapped the fish in leaves that I had put in cool water and added the food to his little bag and he was ready to go.

I know he hates it, but I reminded him to stay on the path, not to talk to strangers, and to pay attention to the things around him. It is a safe place here where we live, but he is my only son.

I waved to him, and watched him vanish over the hill. When he was out of sight, I got ready and set out to go into town. Once there I realized that there was something happening. Everyone was talking about the teacher, Jesus. They said he was nearby on the hill just outside of town. I knew that Obi wouldn't be home for hours and I decided to go and hear this teacher.

I made my way to the top of the hill so that I could hear the words clearly and also could keep an eye on the beach. I looked down and there was Obi with his friends. They were splashing in the water, collecting shells and stones, and I could see he was having fun, so I concentrated on the words of Jesus.

"Blessed are the meek, blessed are the poor,

blessed are the peacemakers, blessed are those who hunger and thirst." That reminded me that I was hungry and I thought of Obi and his lunch. I looked at the beach and couldn't see the boys anywhere. I wondered where they had gone to eat, but reminded myself, he was nearly grown, and I turned back to the teacher.

A man called Andrew was asking how they could feed all these people. He said it would cost a great deal of money to go into town and buy bread. Just then I noticed a lad standing by Andrew and tugging at his sleeve. I recognized Obi and saw him hand Andrew the lunch I had packed. Andrew took it, shrugged his shoulders and gave it to Jesus.

Jesus smiled, and then held up my food and blessed it. "Blessed are you Lord God, king of the universe who brings forth all good things from the earth." I could see that Obi was excited because it is the same grace that we use before each meal. Then the most extraordinary thing happened. As the people were sitting in groups, suddenly there was food being shared. Everyone was eating, talking and enjoying the meal provided.

I got up and hurried home to be there before Obi arrived. When he came in he was very excited. I let him tell the story and then I admitted I had been there too. Obi said that he wanted to hear more from this teacher and learn from him.

After he was in bed, I thought about what he had said. He has always been a determined child, and I could see that he was serious about this, and I was fascinated by this teacher too. In the morning I told Obi that we would both go and hear this man whenever we could.

Obi hugged me and said. "Mother, God was in that place. I could feel it. Could you?"

* * *

Questions for Contemplation or Discussion

1. Can you make any connections between this story and the verse that says Jesus is the bread of life?

2. The disciples didn't see the solution in a boy's lunch. Do our preconceptions limit our understanding of God? In what way?

3. Does this story speak to physical or spiritual needs, or perhaps both?

Emuna
Meaning Faith
II Kings 5; 1-15

Background

Naanam, the commander of the Syrian army, had a disfiguring skin disease. On a raid into Israel he captured a young woman and brought her to his home as a slave for his wife.

* * *

Ah, I enjoy the cool evenings. Sitting in this lovely garden, remembering. I have had a most interesting and wonderful life. Not all of it, but I try and dwell on the good that the Holy One has brought to me.

I was born and raised in a devout Jewish family in Israel. My father was a leader in our community, loved and respected, and my mother was an important influence in our home. She taught all her children the songs of our deliverance, and she taught us to pray. The lighting of the Sabbath candles was a wonderful ritual in our home each Friday evening. Mother taught us all about God and about our deliverance as a people from slavery in Egypt. She told and retold the stories of how God was always with us in our struggles, and how he forgave when we went astray and how he continually called us back when we wandered away. I knew all about the prophets and the healers and the teachers in my country.

Mother always said that we were to be lights in the world. She taught that the light of God shone in our lives when we kept the commandments and lived in kindness and peace. I think she knew that bad things could happen to us for she taught us how to live when we were afraid. We were told to remember the stories of God saving our people when they were slaves in Egypt. She reminded us of God's care in famine and in drought.

When the soldiers came mother hid each of us in a different place and told us to remember the candle of hope and the light that God brings to our lives. I don't know what happened to my family, but I was found by a soldier and taken to the commander of the army. From there, I was taken to their land and given to the wife of the captain of the army to be her slave.

She was a kind mistress and treated me with tenderness. She allowed me to follow my religion and gave me candles and permitted me to light them each Friday night as I ate my supper. I tried to remember all that my mother had taught me and to stay faithful to the God of my people, the one we called Holy One.

All was going fine in our household, although I missed my family and wondered if they were still alive. But things turned bad when Naaman became a leper. It was a tragedy for my owners and was going to change our lives forever. They had tried all the medicines in their country and all kinds of healers and magicians, but the disease was steadily growing worse.

I told my mistress that if only we lived in Israel Naaman could go to the prophet Elijah and he could be cured. She told her husband and messengers were sent. Naaman did not want to follow the instructions of Elijah. He wanted to bath in the clean rivers of this land, not the muddy Jordon. He was also angry that Elijah did not meet him but sent out a messenger. But he did what Elijah said, and he was cured. And again our lives were changed, for Naaman began to ask about the God of Israel.

All my life the light of the candles lit on Friday have been a source of hope for me, and I did my best to remember the faith my mother taught me. I have prayed and sung the songs mother sang. I remember my mother's teaching that God comes to us and brings light into our lives.

The light of joy.
The light of hope.
The light of Love.
The light of peace.

* * *

Questions for Contemplation or Discussion

1. This was an amazing thing for this slave girl to do. She did a very kind thing for the man who was her captor. What led her to do this?

2. Do you think Naaman would have recognized how unusual this act of his slave was?

3. Most healing stories in the Bible state that faith is required to be healed. Naaman did not know the God of Israel, yet he was healed. What could this be saying to us in our multi-cultural world?

Chapter 4
Women Near the Manger

Women Befriending Mary

As I said in my introduction, Ruether and Fiorenza encourage women to look for the missing characters and use our sacred imagination to tell their part in the story. This is what I have done with this often told, much loved story. I have tried to stay faithful to the intent of the stories, and hope these soliloquies add colour and a personal note to your engagement in the Christmas story.

It is an interesting picture that has developed around the Christmas stories. Matthew and Luke are the only two Gospel writers that have a birth narrative for Jesus, and they have little in common in their writings. Christmas pageants, cards and carols, take the two stories and blend them into a very touching scene. However, Luke says nothing about wise men. Matthew doesn't mentions shepherds or a stable, and neither of them talk about three of the women whom I have imagined into the story.

Elizabeth, Mary the mother of Jesus, and Anna exist in the Bible stories, and I have developed a story based on what is written and what I feel they might have thought.

The other three are my creations to tell the story from a woman's perspective. After all, it is a birth narrative and women are the centre of birth stories, and I feel there are missing perspectives in the telling of this pivotal event in history. I hope these new stories add to your enjoyment of this season we call Christmas.

Elizabeth
Relative of Mary
Luke 1: 1-80, 2:1

Background

Elizabeth was of priestly descent and was married to Zechariah, a priest, descended from Aaron the first high priest. Childless into her old age, she gave birth to a son long after menopause. Her son was John the Baptizer, a prophet, who prepared the way for Jesus.

* * *

Such delight I find in my son. What a blessing after I had given up all hope of a child. I remember the day Zechariah came home so exited he could hardly stand still while he explained what had happened. He was unable to speak, but after much acting and writing and guessing, I learned what had happened to him. An angel had appeared and told him we were to have a child and he was to be named John. Zechariah reacted with disbelief and the angel declared he would be mute until the child was named.

I too found it hard to accept but my husband was very happy, very excited and indeed unable to speak. I had no choice but to believe him. But why name him John? First born sons are always given a family name and there is no one named John in our lineage. No wonder Zechariah had questions. I had some of my own.

It would have been nice if an angel had come to me. Why only to Zechariah? I am the one to carry this child—to feed him, bathe him, and nurture him till he becomes a man. But I had to figure it out from a man who couldn't speak and couldn't contain his joy. Such is the life of a woman.

It wasn't long until I knew it was true. My body began to change. I couldn't eat in the morning. Such a terrible feeling, almost every morning for months. But that passed and I began to marvel at this wonderful event and to prepare for my child.

And here I am. Holding my young son in my arms. Such joy, such a blessing. As I sit like this, my baby fed and content, I can't help but think of Mary. We had such a wonderful time together. When she arrived she was exhausted from her journey, she was afraid and uncertain of her future. She had a visit from an angel and learned she was to bear a special child. I rejoiced with her. She was betrothed to Joseph, the carpenter, and did not know how to tell him what had happened. We have always been close and so she came at once to me.

As we sewed for our coming babies, I was able

to calm her fears about her pregnancy and the time of delivery. I assured her that the midwife in Nazareth was a wonderful woman and she would help her through it all. I also reminded her that Joseph was a good man and he would do the right thing by her. By the time she left, she was much calmer and looking forward to what God had called her to do. Joseph too had a visit from an angel, and when he understood, he came to get her and take her home. He could have put her away, banished her from the town, or stoned her to death outside the walls. But he is going to honour their betrothal and marry her. Such a good husband and father he will be.

It must be close to her time now. How good for her to be surrounded by friends and family in Nazareth. They will accept what has happened when they see the two of them married and happy together. Each new baby is greeted with joy by all the women in our villages. And it will be a boy; that means even greater celebration.

I am sure that Joseph has been making the most beautiful cradle ever to hold a baby. He must be so happy. Joseph is not young and to marry such a beautiful, clever and bright young woman is something he can brag about in the marketplace. And when his son arrives, they will be so happy together. They will be good parents, I know, raising the boy to follow his father's trade, and he will be taught our faith by two devout parents. They are very lucky, but so is the child they will have.

I look at my son and think about his future. He will be a priest in the temple, just as his father and grandfather have been. I shall teach him well and keep a proper home for him. Between us we will raise him to be a God-fearing man and a credit to his lineage. I'll make sure that he grows up knowing Mary's son. They are both special, chosen by God for great things and they need to know each other and share their lives together. Chosen by God. Imagine it. I wonder what that will mean as they grow into men. Time will tell and only the holy one knows what will happen.

I am old and will not live to see John grow up, but Mary is young. She will have such joy in watching her son grow in wisdom and stature as he becomes a man, following in his father's trade.

No matter how many other children she has, this baby will always be special to her. The first born son is always close to his mother. Mary is so blessed to have a son who will care for her in her old age. We are such fortunate women to be chosen by God to bear these sons who have such promise for their lives.

God is good. Blessed by the name of the Holy One of Israel.

* * *

Questions for Contemplation or Discussion

1. How do you think Mary has been treated by the church over the centuries?

2. Elizabeth, as an older women, helps Mary. Who have been the women in your life who have been mentors and teachers for you?

3. Who do you think young women today have as role models? In your opinion, are they mostly positive or negative examples of womanhood.

Gabriella
Wife of the Innkeeper
Means Messenger of God
Luke 2:1-7

Background

There is no mention of such a woman in the Biblical story, but our imaginations can quite realistically develop such a person. To see her as a midwife in the story is an easy step once she is part of the scene.

* * *

At times I get so cross with my husband. All he thinks about is squeezing out the last shekel from every traveller who comes to the door. He knows that people have been forced by government decree to come here to Bethlehem. They have travelled for days and are tired and at their wits end. Most are poor and have little money for rooms or food.

My heart went out to that last couple he started to turn away.

"No room," he said.

But there was that small room at the back where they would have been able to sleep. He knew they couldn't pay what he was asking so he was turning them out into the night. She looked ready to deliver her baby any moment, and how young she was, and exhausted. She has probably been sleeping in ditches all the way here. And I wonder when she last had a hot meal. I stated they could not be turned away.

"There is no room," he yelled again.

In desperation I mentioned the stable. She smiled and said that it would be just fine. Her voice trembled and her smile was forced.

Her husband asked if she was sure, and she said, "Yes, we will be alright Joseph. You know we are in the tender keeping of the Holy One of Israel."

So I led them to the stable. He fussed about making a soft place for her to lie down and put his cloak on the hay for her to rest upon.

As she lay down I heard a faint gasp and she grabbed her belly. I went to her at once and quickly saw that her pains had started. I have delivered a lot of babies and I could tell her labour was well advanced. What an ordeal it must have been for her. Riding on that donkey and in labour. She must have not made a sound, as I could see that her husband had no idea. I told her to rest and I would be back soon.

At the inn, I gathered up some blankets to keep her warm and more comfortable. Then I went to my trunk to get the swaddling bands I keep for my deliveries. I warmed some broth, and got bread, cheese, and milk and headed back to the stable. I sat with her while she ate what she could. She was very grateful. I told Joseph that for a few coins he could get something to eat at the inn. He left, looking helpless and glad of a reason to leave.

She told me he was a carpenter and I thought, *he'll be no help at all.* A shepherd might have some idea of what to do, but a carpenter? He's better off at the inn. She seemed comfortable and so I went back to get some things for the birth: warm oil to rub on her belly to sooth and relax her, a tea made of herbs that will ease her pain a little, and a small lamp for some light. Flames and stables aren't a good idea, but I would need some light. Also a basin of warm water to wash the baby. She says it is a boy she is carrying; she was very certain about that. I tried to remind her that girl babies are born too, but she insisted it was a boy.

I thought that was everything I'd need. My husband, the greedy business man, started grumbling because I wouldn't be there to do his bidding, but I simply said that I was needed in the stable and left.

I can't ever remember the sky being as bright as it was that night. I didn't need the lamp after all. I had never seen the stars so dazzling. They seemed close enough to touch, and as they twinkled they seemed to be dancing. What a glorious night. Then I heard a lovely sound. Like music. Beautiful music. It seemed to be coming from the hills where the shepherds rest at night. I've rarely heard shepherds sing and certainly not like that. It sounded heavenly. That night turned out to be unusual in many ways. I had never delivered a baby in a stable before. I was so glad that it all turned out well and there was a happy ending.

She was right. It was a boy. A beautiful boy,

strong and healthy. She was so brave. Hardly a whimper out of her. She seemed to be singing one of the Psalms, but I was so busy I couldn't make out which one. But it brought her comfort and so that was a good thing. Joseph was just outside the stable door, and he was very relieved when I told him all was well and he had a son.

When I left them they looked very, very happy. The baby was sleeping in the manger; Mary was resting on her blankets, and Joseph was standing guard over them. Even the animals seemed to be quieter than usual. The sky was still bright but I didn't hear the music. Maybe I had imagined it. Then I saw something coming over the hill. Many shepherds were coming this way toward the stable. I thought I should head them off, but as they came closer, Joseph welcomed them and invited them in. How strange.

One thing I was sure of. When the story got around the village about this birth in the stable, the women at the well would have something new to talk about. This would put talk of the messiah to rest for a while. A baby born in a stable and shepherds visiting.

That was enough to keep tongues wagging for weeks.

* * *

Questions for Contemplation or Discussion

1. Do you find it plausible that someone might have been there to help Mary?

2. Suppose that in later years she heard about Jesus and connected him to his birth. What do you think she would be feeling?

3. How might she have been supportive of Mary at the end of Jesus' life?

Adira

Meaning Strong
Wife of a Shepherd

Luke 2: 8-20

Background

While there is no mention of the wives of the shepherds in the biblical material, it is within reason that such women existed. This story is to help us see the birth narrative through a different, yet imaginary, set of eyes and experience.

* * *

My husband left for his turn in the fields with the sheep to care for them overnight. It was his usual time to go, and I was always prepared for this time alone. It gave me time to think, to pray, and to ponder the ways of the world and the ways of God. Our people had waited for generations for the coming of the Messiah—the One who was to lead our people to new hope and freedom. The yoke of Rome was a heavy one, and we were a tired and discouraged people.

I thought a great deal about these things when I

was alone. My husband had almost given up hope. He felt that God had forgotten us, or was angry for some reason and had withdrawn his care. I could not believe that God would ever forget us, and I was among those who thought that our deliverance must be coming soon. For we had borne so much and our children needed to grow up free and happy and secure.

I went to bed and slept the sleep of the exhausted. I didn't hear him coming up the path, but when he burst through the door I knew he was home. He was singing a Psalm of deliverance at the top of his lungs, shouting hallelujah and praise God. At first I thought he must be drunk, but he was a man who had never been drunk since our marriage. I wondered if he was having some kind of fit, but he seemed to be alright, except for the noise and his wild story.

His voice was strong, his eyes clear, I might even say they were shining with joy or something. His step was steady and he seemed delirious with happiness. He grabbed my hands and began twirling me around the room, singing God's praises all the time. I tried to quiet him before he woke the children, the animals, and the neighbours.

Finally he ran out of energy and fell into a chair. I gave him some food and waited for him to explain. He took a deep breath and gently held one of my hands. Then slowly, almost reverently, he began to explain.

"I have seen him. The messiah. Out in the fields there were angels filling the sky and they told us to go to Bethlehem to find him. He was in a stable with his mother and father, just as the angels said. And he is the most beautiful child I have ever seen. No really, he was. I know he was just an infant, but he looked at us with such peace and wisdom in his eyes. He seemed to be both young and ancient. I tell you Adira, I have seen the Messiah. Our deliverer is here."

I listened respectfully and finally got him to go to bed and rest. Then I tried to make sense of all this. I began to wonder what the neighbours would think about his story. At once I felt uncertain. To keep it all quiet would be the best thing for everyone. The people liked to talk, and this would make a wonderful story to tell at the well, and the inn. I can hear them saying, "Do you know that shepherd, the one who has gone off his head? He claims to have seen a new baby, and that he is our long-awaited Messiah."

Then they would laugh because the baby was born in a barn. What a terrible place to give birth. I wonder if she was alone there, without a midwife or a friend to hold her hand. She must have been very frightened and very brave. Thinking about it now, I ask myself, "What kind of baby is born in a barn?" Not a messiah, and that is a fact. And everyone who hears the story will know that. I can understand him being born in Jerusalem, or Herod's palace. But a barn?

Never!

And yet . . . he was so sure. I have never seen him filled with such joy. He has always been a good man, and faithful to God, but tonight he was in some kind of spiritual glory. Part of me wants the story to just go away, be forgotten, die with the sunlight. But, what if it could be true? What if that infant is the messiah? Our freedom would become a reality. The prince of peace would be among us. If only it has really happened. The waiting would be over and joy would come in the morning. Not just to Bethlehem but to all our people.

Please God, let it be so.

Let it be so.

* * *

Question for Contemplation or Discussion

1.   Can you imagine the next few days in Bethlehem as word gets around the town? What might the most common reaction have been?

2.   In what ways might this experience have changed the shepherds? Do you think it was all forgotten in the years ahead when they heard no news of the deliverer?

3.   Have you ever received news that changed your life or the way you saw the world?

Mary
Mother of the Infant Jesus
Luke 1:26-56 2:1-38

Background

The information concerning Mary has been told in song, sermon and art since the beginning of the Christian church. This interpretation of the birth of Jesus uses imagination to fill in the gaps in the story.

* * *

At last it is quiet. I was so tired when we arrived in Bethlehem. It was a struggle for us to keep up with the others. I could not ride for very long, as it was so uncomfortable, but I was not able to walk quickly either. Gradually, a group of us gathered—some elderly, some with walking challenges, and we formed our own little community as we travelled. It took us a few days longer, and so I was worried about finding any place where we could stay.

I remember the messenger saying, "Do not be afraid." I tried, but most of the last year has been filled with fear. I worried that Joseph would put me away, banish me, or even have me stoned. The law gave him that power. But he too had a special messenger and he honoured our betrothal.

I worried about our long journey—many days on the road, long hours trying to sit on the donkey's back, or walking beside Joseph. And there was always the fear of bandits and robbers, but we were with others. I wondered where we would stay. Bethlehem is a small village and there were so many people going there for the census. But whenever the fear threatened to take over, I remembered that the Holy One is our refuge and our strength.

But still, we were disappointed when the innkeeper said there was no room. The fear welled up again and I wondered where my child would be born. The wife of the innkeeper was a great help when she suggested the stable and she did her best to get us comfortable. What a blessing she was when I went into the last stages of labour. I had been having contractions for hours along the road, but said nothing to Joseph. He would have panicked, as he was so worried about my safety on the road. Sleeping in the straw in a stable was a big improvement over Joseph's cloak and the ditch.

But my son is here now, and we are both doing fine. What a joy he will be. It feels odd to give him the name of Jesus. We give our children family names, or names that have great meaning for us. Sometimes we give our children names that express our hopes and dreams for them. Perhaps his name, Jesus, meaning

God saves, is his destiny. I try not to worry about his future, but I guess every mother worries about her children, even when they aren't born in such unusual circumstances.

But after all the fears and worries, here he is in my arms. A beautiful baby boy, just as we were promised. After we were settled by the mid-wife and she left us to be a family together for the first time, some shepherds came to the door of the stable. They said they heard angels telling of the birth of a baby in Bethlehem and they were told to travel from the hills to see the child. They quietly and reverently knelt at the manger. I had always known this child I carried was not going to live the ordinary life of a carpenter, but at that moment I realized how special he was.

They spoke words from our prophet Isaiah. "He shall be called wonderful, counsellor and king of kings." And I began to wonder. What kind of a king will you be my little one? I do not think you will ride on a great white steed, leading armies and wielding a sword. Besides, that kind of a king would not be born in a stable, but in a palace. He would not have straw for a bed and animals for companions. And then I remember other words: wounded for our transgressions, bruised for our iniquity, chastised for our misdeeds. I wonder what it all means.

But the future lies ahead. For now you are my child. My gift from God, and when the time comes

God will show you the way. It is my task to teach you. Teach you love, and peace, and justice, and the story of your people. This will help you find the strength to be the man God has chosen you to be.

* * *

Questions for Contemplation or Discussion

1. Can you imagine what it must have been like for Mary at that time in her life?

2. Do you think the way we tell the story gives credit to Mary's strength, faith and courage?

3. Do you have a picture of Mary, or a painting, or image that has meaning for you? Think about its meaning, and share it with the group.

Anna

Old Woman in the Temple

Luke 2: 36-38

Background

Anna is the elderly woman in the temple when Mary and Joseph take Jesus there for the purification ceremony that followed the birth of a child. She was a devout woman who had lived in the temple since she became a widow, many years before. She, along with Simeon, was there to greet this holy child.

* * *

Oh, these old bones. Sometimes it is very difficult to get up from my sleeping mat and get moving in the morning. I have my simple breakfast and then go about my day. I love the temple spaces in the early morning. It is quiet and peaceful. I find it easier to sense God's presence in these cool, quiet times. As the day unfolds, the temple gets busy and noisy and smelly. All the animals and birds for the sacrifices are bleating or cooing. The sellers are calling out to people and the undercurrent of chatter as the pilgrims arrive and try to find their way about creates a din that echoes from the stonework. Then there are the teachers with their students, all talking at once. I wonder who is listening? Hmmm. Maybe nobody but the Holy One.

I remember the day well. It was an ordinary day, or so I thought, until my eye caught sight of them. I saw them slowly entering the temple. She seemed very young, quiet and shy, yet with a dignity that only those who know God seem to have. He was a big man, strong yet gentle in the way he was caring for her and the baby. He seemed very protective of them.

I was drawn to them, but I stayed out of sight behind a pillar. The priests tolerate me, because I help to look after the poor and the sick. I try to keep them out of their way, so they are not bothered by these, the least of God's children. I didn't want anything to spoil this moment so I stayed hidden.

Simeon, one of the oldest of the teachers in the temple, approached them. And just as he always did, he started to speak the holy words. He laid his hand on the baby's head, and said that he could now die in peace for he had seen the promise of the Lord fulfilled. He, like everyone else was waiting for the Messiah, and I wondered if he thought this simple family was bringing to the temple the anointed one for a special blessing. But to me it appeared to be simply the usual presentation after birth.

When all the holy words were said, and the holy ritual done, they were leaving the temple. The mother spotted me by the pillar and beckoned me to her. As I came near, I had a very real sense of the presence of the sacred. The Holy One was very close and I realized this was a very sacred moment. Simeon was right. This was the chosen one of God.

I slowly approached the family, and she held out the baby to me. These old arms had hardly ever held an infant. And here I stood, taking in my arms this chosen one of Israel. Tenderly and very carefully, I held him close to my heart. He smelled so sweet, and looked so peaceful. My heart was pounding in my chest, and I could hardly breathe. As I looked at him, his infant eyes seemed very wise. He looked as if he carried in his very being all the weight of humanity.

As I held him, I could hear in my head the words of the prophets. *A man of sorrows, acquainted with grief. Led as a lamb to the slaughter.* I could hear the jeers of an angry crowd and the sound of a hammer. Then I thought I heard thunder, and the rush of the wind and driving rain. And for a moment I heard a terrible sound, like the tearing asunder of a great divide. I shuddered, and it was gone. There was nothing but these two parents, an infant in my arms, and the bustle of the temple.

I didn't realize I was crying until she reached out as she took her child back and she gently wiped the tears from these old cheeks. Then they turned and, without a word, slowly walked away from me and out into the streets. As I watched them go, I wondered who would be there to wipe away her tears in the years ahead.

The ways of the Holy One are wondrous and mysterious. But we are never alone. The God of Abraham and of Sarah will always be our refuge and our strength.   Thanks be to God.

* * *

Questions for contemplation or discussion

1. Can you surmise why Simeon recognized the baby as the hoped for Messiah?

2.   What is your response to Anna's words in this imaginative story?

3.   Do we notice God's presence in the ordinary? Give an example.

Miriamne
Wife of Herod
Matthew 2: 1-12

Backgound

Miriamne was of royal lineage and was married to Herod in a marriage arranged by her mother. She bore Herod two sons and two daughters. It is said that she was very beautiful and that Herod loved her deeply. But he was such a tyrant and so afraid of enemies that he did not completely trust her. According to history, she was executed likely at Herod's command but he deeply grieved her loss.

* * *

I've been married to Herod for many years now and I look back on them in both happiness and horror. We had four children, and they were the joy of my life. I tried to raise them to be kind and loving, decent human beings. But it was very difficult, for their father was a tyrant. He would be kind and good one day, and the next, threatening all of us, accusing us of tyranny and plotting against him. There were times when I feared for the life of my sons.

He was a powerful ruler and did many great

113

things. He enlarged and beautified the temple in Jerusalem. Were the people happy about their wonderful temple? No. They grumbled and complained that he had profaned the sacred house of their strange God. He built forts to guard against invaders; he developed an outstanding port at Caesarea. Trade had never been so profitable before this port was opened to the great cargo ships of the sea. But no one understood him or appreciated his greatness. He became more and more isolated and fearful.

One day three very interesting visitors arrived at the palace. They came from far, far away. As we entertained them at dinner, we learned they were following a star that was travelling across the sky. They said it foretold the birth of a great king and they were travelling to pay homage to him. Needing a rest and hoping to find him in the palace, they stopped here, but we knew of no king except Herod. I could see that he was greatly upset.

Herod sent them away to rest and called for all his advisors. They searched their star charts, read all the scrolls and writings they could think of. One of them remembered the prophets of old saying that a ruler would arise out of Bethlehem. Herod went to the visitors and told them of the saying. He asked them to return and tell him where they found the new king and said that he wanted to go and worship him as well.

They left and went on their way to the village of Bethlehem. But they never returned. Herod waited, becoming more and more agitated. He finally became enraged when he realize they were not coming back to tell him what they had found.

In his anger and fear for his throne, he was determined to get rid of this threat. He decreed that all boy babies were to be killed. I risked my life in doing so, but I went to him, to try and stop this horrible edict.

He wouldn't listen. I tried everything I could think of. Promises, bribes, feminine whiles, flattery, but nothing could reach his mind in his delusional state.

I shut myself in my room, and tried not to think of the horror that was happening just a few miles away.

I have heard of a story of a Pharaoh of Egypt who tried the same tactic, and it did not stop the loss of his slaves and his kingdom. I am sure that this won't stop the God of these Hebrews if this baby's future is the will of their God.

I feel that I have gone too far this time, and my own life is in danger. Herod can have me killed and I think that will be my fate. If it is, I know that at least I died trying to do the right thing. What evil overcomes men when they have such power?

If there is such a child born, I pray to the God of the Hebrews that somehow he will be spared. This is a land of such promise. It needs a ruler who will have the needs of the people and this country foremost in his mind. Herod is not that man. He will lead to despair and destruction.

May a new king arise who will lead the people in justice, so that all may live in peace.

* * *

Questions for Contemplation or Discussion

1. Can you make any connections between the two stories of the slaughter of innocent babies? (Reference above, and Exodus 1: 15-22)

2. Do you think there is truth in the saying that power corrupts and absolute power corrupts absolutely?

3, What rulers, past or present, can you name who ruled with justice and compassion?

Chapter 5
Women Who Knew Jesus

Disciples and Followers

These six women were a part of the ministry of Jesus in different ways. Salome (in some scholars interpretation) and Peter's mother-in-law had family who were disciples of Jesus and were very close to him. Jesus' sisters are mentioned in Matthew's gospel, but there is no information about them. There is a book called the Urantia which names Jesus' brothers and sisters. This book originated in Chicago sometime between 1924 and 1955. The authorship is unknown. I have chosen to name his sister Bina, which means wisdom. As I feel my way into her life, wisdom seems a good choice for a name for her.

Mary of Bethany is well known by readers of the Bible. The two I have named Marnie and Veronica are known in scripture by the illness that brought them to Jesus.

I have often wondered and wished that somewhere original writings by the women who were a part of this story of Jesus will be found.

I know that will probably never happen as most women could neither read nor write at that time. In fact not all men had those skills either at this time in history. Yet I still wonder, and so my imagination takes over and these women come alive in my heart and mind as spirit sisters.

I hope they might speak to you as you hear or read their stories.

Marnie
Meaning Rejoice
A Bent Over Woman
Luke 13: 10-17

Background

Jesus met this woman in the synagogue on the Sabbath. Her crippled condition is often seen as physical, but Luke says a spirit of infirmity. That might mean she was bent over, not with a deformity, but with oppression or rejection.

* * *

My childhood was typical of a girl in my village. We played and helped our mothers as we learned the skills needed to be a wife and mother. I often wished that I could go to school as my brothers did, but was laughed at when I asked about it. I envied them as they learned to read and to study the Torah. Why couldn't I learn as well? I was quick to pick things up and I had many questions. No one would even listen to them and certainly not give me any answers. At times I hated being a girl. I stopped asking questions, but they did not go away. As I grew older and saw more of the world, I had more and more questions.

The fact that no one would talk to me about my questions, not even the women, made me very sad. At times my longing to learn seemed like a heavy burden that I was forced to carry day and night.

Time went on and I grew to be a young woman of marriageable age. My parents tried to arrange my marriage. As they talked to the young man's parents, my reputation as a trouble maker made it very difficult for them. Since they were reluctant to consent to their son being tied to a woman such as I, they did not offer a dowry my parents would accept. My parents were looking out for me, in case I was divorced. They were losing hope for a suitable marriage for me.

Years went by and soon I was past the age when anyone that I would agree to marry would even consider it. And so I was at home, caring for my aging parents. The burdens I carried became heavier and pressed down on my very being. My parents died and I was now completely alone.

To the village children I was a crazy woman. To the men I was uppity and self-important. To the women I was a mystery and a disgrace to womanhood. And so I lived a life of solitude, not by choice, but by being excluded from society. Even at the synagogue no one ever invited me to their gatherings after worship. The well was a place to share friendship for the women, but eyes were averted when I arrived to get my water, and conversation stopped.

Every day I woke up sad and I went to bed at night sad. It was all weighing my spirits down and I saw no hope for the years that lay ahead.

One day, at the market, I heard the people talking about a new rabbi. He was different from our rabbi they said. He spoke of love, peace, hope and a new life lived in the light of the love of God.

I thought about it for a long time and then decided to risk going to hear him. The crowd was huge at the synagogue, but I was finally noticed by him. He looked at me and smiled and called me to him. His eyes looked at me and I felt that he could see everything that was bending me over. He gently spoke and told me that I was freed from all that troubled me. Immediately I felt the heaviness gone. I knew that I was not crazy, that I was a valued human being. And I smiled a genuine smile of happiness for the first time in many years.

The officials at the synagogue began to grumble and accuse him of breaking God's commandments. He looked at them and his eyes lost their compassion and became darker and cold. Then he told them that they would look after a donkey in distress on the Sabbath and I was a daughter of Abraham and deserved no less.

I was changed. I no longer felt I needed to apologize for being myself. Things changed a little in the community, but I was still on the edges of their society. But now it didn't matter. The rabbi had said I was a daughter of the covenant too and that blessing would be mine for as long as I lived. I am no longer sad. I greet each day with hope. And I recite the words of the singer of Psalms,"God has girded me with strength, and made my way safe."

Thanks be to God.

* * *

Questions for Contemplation or Discussion

1.   Jesus gave precedence to a woman over religious regulations. How do you feel about his actions?

2.   Marnie is portrayed in this reading as a woman who tried to live a life that was counter-culture. How acceptable is that in to-day's society?

3.   What restrictions might bend women over to-day ?

Veronica
The Bleeding Woman
Mark 5: 25-34

Background

There is within the Catholic tradition a Saint Veronica. She was a pious woman of Jerusalem in the first century who was healed by touching the hem of Jesus' garment. There is another story that says a woman named Veronica followed Christ to the cross and gave him her veil to wipe his face as he carried his cross. It was said to bear the likeness of his face. This scene is the VI station on the Via Dolorosa. If we assume this is the same woman a story of devotion comes to light.

* * *

I could think of nothing else to do. It was a great risk to do what I had planned, but I was desperate. I had been bleeding, as a woman does monthly, but for twelve years. It began at the time when I first started my womanly courses. There were a few days when I was not bleeding, but that was of no account. The law said that I remained ritually unclean for seven days after the bleeding stopped. Under this law, I was unclean all the time.

That made my life unbearable. I lived with my parents but when this bleeding continued they found it very hard and tragic. The rules made it impossible to have me in their house. These laws of impurity shut me away from real contact for most of my days. No one could sit on a stool on which I had been sitting. And so I had my own stool. I had my own dishes and spoon, a bowl in which to wash. I washed my own clothes, bed linens, everything for no one could touch anything that I had touched. If they did, they too would become unclean until the evening of the same day. They could not touch me either; I was never hugged, no one could brush my hair, lace my garments, hold my hand. My parents could not live like this and so they turned me out and found me a tiny space in which to stay. They came to see me and to give me money so that I could live. But we talked through the doorway and they never came in to my little house, which was just a room with a door and one window.

Life was barren, cold, empty. I tried the doctors and all that did was make me poor. They could not help me. How could they, when they wouldn't get near me or touch me? They told me to drink this tea or that potion or use this salve. Nothing changed. I had to do something or I would die of a broken heart.

I had heard of the healer called Jesus and I was determined to find him. But then what? I thought about it for a long time and finally decided on a plan. I would dress very plainly and hide my face. Hardly anyone knew me, but I didn't want to risk being seen and recognized. I would quietly come up to him from behind and touch his garment. I knew that he was a man of God and surely God would come to my aid. As I looked to the hills and prayed, I felt at peace, and when Jesus came near my place, I was ready.

I dressed with care and slipped away in the early hours of the day to go to the place where he was to come and teach. When he arrived I knew him at once. There was such strength in his walk. Such power in his face. Such gentleness in his voice and such compassion in his look.

I was at the edge of the crowd, but slowly worked my way nearer to him, being very careful not to touch anyone. As he turned to face the great mass of people, I reached out and touched the hem of his robe. At once I felt a peace and a strength that I had not known for years.

He spoke, "Who touched me?"

The disciples scoffed, but I knew that he had felt my presence. I threw myself at his feet and confessed. He smiled at me and said that my belief had been the source of my healing. "Go in peace, daughter," he said in blessing.

I decided that I would follow him and learn more about him and his teaching. And I did, listening and learning and helping the women disciples when I could. And I was there when he was arrested. I followed the jeering crowd as he carried his cross along the streets to the hill of crucifixion. He stumbled and I could see the blood and tears on his face. I gave him a piece of clean cloth and he wiped his brow. As he handed it back, he smiled and said, "Thank you Daughter." He knew me. I could tell. He remembered and once again I received his blessing. In spite of the horror of that time, once again I felt at peace.

* * *

Questions for Contemplation or Discussion

1. Have you heard of Saint Veronica? Her feast day is July 12 and she is the patron saint of laundry workers and photographers. Do you have any thoughts or comments?

2. What is the significance of this story for women?

3. Deep inside of each woman, there is the memory of a little girl. Can you remember her? What was she like? What would you tell her today if you could talk to her?

Bina

Meaning wisdom

A sister of Jesus
Matthew 13: 53-58

Background

Many believe that Jesus had no brothers and sisters, and that these mentioned in Matthew and in Mark, were either half-siblings from a previous marriage of Joseph, or his cousins. But many others believe that the marriage of Mary and Joseph was normal in every way, including the conception of other children. Bina, in this story, is the sister born after Jesus.

* * *

I loved my older brother, we all did. But at times it was hard to be his younger sister. Jesus never got into mischief the way we did. The rest of us would go into the orchard and eat the fruit straight from the trees. The figs tasted wonderful, warm with the sun, sweet and delicious. But that meant less for the family or to sell at the market. When we went to pick the wild berries, we got very hungry and thirsty. It was tempting to eat some to ease our thirst. The trouble was I couldn't eat just one. Since I had to bring my basket home filled to the brim, the more I ate, the longer I had to stay and pick. I never saw Jesus eat even one berry when he went with us. So his basket was always filled before the rest of ours. An ordinary brother would have run home and gloated over how fast he could pick. But not Jesus. He dumped some of his into my basket and then went to work to fill his up again. I loved how kind he was, how he never got me into trouble, even when he might have, but sometimes his goodness made me feel worse when I was naughty.

I remember the years we lived in Egypt. The memories are not very clear, as I was very young. But Jesus was always helping father or mother. She found it very hard to go to market, as it was all so strange, but Jesus went with her every time. He was such a beautiful child, that people stopped to admire him, and that made things easier for mother. Every day when father was finished working in the shop, without being asked, Jesus would go and sweep the floor and put all the tools away. He even oiled them for father when he was a bit older. The rest of us had to be reminded to help and sometimes we grumbled because we would rather play. But not Jesus.

The story we heard about our going to Egypt made us realize that he was a very special baby. They went there to save his life and we didn't return to

Nazareth until it was safe for him to grow up there. Our lives were pretty ordinary except for Jesus and his faultless behaviour.

I was married young, as were my sisters, and my brothers found work in the village, fishing, farming or selling goods in the market stalls. Jesus worked with father, and was a very good carpenter. He took over the shop after father died and he looked after mother. Not long after we were at a wedding in Cana, he came to our brother Jude and said, "I am going away. The shop and the work there are now your responsibility. And you must care for mother, for you are the next oldest son." Then he kissed us all good-bye and was gone.

We heard of him often and wondered why he was doing what he did; living as a travelling prophet and teacher. He had gathered some disciples around him and they were becoming famous and people were following him. We heard stories of him healing people and feeding a crowd from a boy's lunch. I know mother tried to hide it from us, but the people of Nazareth chased him away one day. I often wondered why they would do that, he was so kind and gentle.

And now in just three years, it has all come to an end. He was crucified on that hill in Jerusalem and mother has gone to live with John, his disciple. There were stories that some of the followers had seen him and he visited with his disciples a couple of times.

Until I see him myself, I am going to go on grieving for my brother. He was very special and I loved him with all my heart. I am not going to get my hopes up, as no one survives being crucified. And yet, mother said that God cared for his own, and nothing was beyond God's power. I wonder, and hope, and carry on with my life.

* * *

Questions for Contemplation or Discussion

1.   Have you given much thought to Jesus' sisters and brothers? Does it make any difference to you if there were siblings?

2.   Can you imagine Bina in any stories of Jesus' life? What role would you see her playing?

3.   What is it like to have someone held up before you as better than you? Have you ever heard your parents say, "Why can't you be more like . . .?" What does that do to a child?

Tibi

Meaning my heart
Mother-in-law of Peter
Matthew 8:14-15

Background

There are two women in this story; neither is named. We do not know if Peter's wife was alive or not. Is it possible that she too joined the women who followed Jesus? Grandma may be left at home with the children and angry that her daughter followed her head-strong husband, leaving her home and children. Tibi may have been very angry and resentful.

* * *

I thought my daughter Tam, married well. Peter was a fisherman and he had a thriving business. He was a big man, strong and hard-working. He and his brother Andrew were in business together, and they made a good team. They were fishermen and as such were bold, brash, hard-headed and uncouth. They dressed poorly and of course smelled of fish. But he cared about my daughter and loved his children.

I was grateful to him when my husband died and he invited me into his home. It was a good arrangement. There were my grandchildren and they were a boisterous group of children. Peter just laughed at their misdeeds and all the discipline fell to my daughter. We did our best to raise them properly, but it was challenging. I was able to help with the washing, cleaning and the meals and she could spend time with her children. Peter was away much of the day, fishing or at the markets, selling the catch, and when he came home, his loud voice and laughter filled the house. I don't mind happiness and joy, but he laughed for all the wrong reasons.

One day he didn't come home. Not for his supper, not as darkness fell and not all night. Tam was worried sick and in the morning she went searching for him. At the shore where the boats tied up for the night, she looked for him. His boat was there, but neither he nor Andrew were in sight. She asked of the other fishermen and they said that yesterday, a man came by, talked to them for a while, and they just left everything and went with him.

Tam learned where they were and went to find them. Late that afternoon she came back to the house. She looked different. Her face had lost its harried look, she was smiling and seemed completely calm. She sat me down and said she had something to tell me.

Well! I was completely in shock. She had listened to this teacher and had become mesmerized by his message. She was going to join the band that followed him. She said there were other women joining as well, and they were going to help this rabbi and his disciples in any way they could.

Great! That left me here with the children, the house and all the work. How was I to feed and clothe and teach these children? Was I supposed to do all the work and go fishing? I went and talked to the rabbi and he said he would help me. He found a man who was a good fisherman but had no boat. We agreed that he would use Peter's boat, give me a portion of the catch each day, both to feed us and to sell, and he would pay rent for the boat.

So there I was. It was all too much. And I was hurt and angry. How could they do this? Just up and leave it all to me? The pain and anger boiled inside of me, until I became ill. I left the two oldest in charge and took to my bed. I swore I was never getting up again.

When I heard a commotion in the house, I wondered what now? Then I heard the children crying, "Mummy, Daddy," and I guessed they were home. Suddenly a man I had never seen was in my room.

He sat on a stool by my bed and looked deeply into my eyes. He spoke my name in such a gentle, caring voice. He then began to talk to me about his mission in life. As I listened, the headache disappeared, the anger slipped away and I was filled with a peace and joy that was new to me. It was wonderful. Suddenly I had energy, I had a purpose and I had a job to do.

I got up and went to the kitchen and started to get a meal ready for my family. And that family now included this teacher, prophet and healer. I understood Peter and Tam's actions now, and I was glad that I could look after this house, family and business and free them to be followers of this holy man. How could a few minutes with Jesus have changed me so completely? I'll never understand, but it doesn't matter.

Life is now filled with meaning and I am content.

* * *

Questions for Contemplation or Discussion

1. Share your thoughts about this imaginative background story to the healing of this woman.

2. How do you feel about the inference that the miracle here was a change of heart and mind for Tibi?

3. What can we as women of to-day learn from this story?

Mary of Bethany
Anointing of Jesus
John 12: 1-8

Background

Each of the Gospels tells a story of Jesus being anointed by a woman in someone's house. The details vary in each telling but the heart of the story is the same. A woman in her total devotion to Jesus pours out a vial of expensive oil and anoints Jesus. I have chosen the story in John, as this Mary, the sister of Martha and Lazarus, is familiar to us.

* * *

Martha and I lived with our brother Lazarus. He took the responsibility of caring for us very seriously.We lived happily together, three very different people, but respectful of each other, most of the time. Lazarus provided for us, but Martha and I each did something to add to our household income.

Martha was a wonderful cook and she loved doing it. She made extra bread and honey cakes and some of our neighbours bought them from her. I loved to weave and sew and sold some cloaks and tunics.

We never asked each other about the money and

just put it into the jar where we kept it for food.

I don't know why I did it, but I always kept a few small coins for myself and placed them in a small jar in my room. I had no definite plans for this money —perhaps for my old age. I really didn't know, but I just felt that I needed to put aside some money that was my own.

The teacher Jesus was a dear friend of ours and came often to our house. I loved to sit near him and listen to his stories and his teaching about God and the kingdom. He was so wise and he talked as if he knew God intimately. He never dismissed me or my questions. I was a serious, thoughtful child and that didn't change when I was a woman and still full of questions. Many people tired of me asking why, or what if, or how come, but Jesus never did. He was patient and kind and he seemed to enjoy our talks.

As the months passed, I sensed a change in him. He became quieter, more thoughtful and at times he even seemed sad. I wondered if it was because the temple authorities were finding fault with him and he was becoming alarmed about the future. But he did not seem to be worried or afraid. Sad is the best way I can describe it.

I loved him dearly and I wondered what I could do for him. I thought for a very long time and then it came to me. When a guest came to a home, it was a sign of respect to wash his feet and anoint his head with oil. Jesus had been at our home so often that he felt more like family than a guest and this custom had slipped from our practice. I decided that is what I could do to show my respect, admiration and love.

I took my coins and added them to the total amount of the last two cloaks I had sold. I was surprised at how much it was. I went to the market, with a lovely alabaster vial I had and bought the best nard I could and filled my little bottle. I hid it safely away.

The next time Jesus and the disciples came I waited until they were finished their meal and were at the table on their cushions just talking. I slipped into the room and knelt at Jesus feet. I broke the top off the vial and poured the oil on his feet. Then I dried them with my hair. I ignored the grumbling of Judas, but Jesus didn't. Jesus told him to leave me alone. Jesus seemed to understand my need to express my devotion and he accepted my gift.

The perfume filled the house. It drifted into every corner and made its presence known. As I knelt there I thought that is just like the love of God. Once the perfume was released nothing could put it back in the bottle. It was present everywhere just like God's love. Once you feel it, and notice it, it is everywhere. You can't put a limit on it. It spreads into every corner of our lives and changes everything.

When Jesus entered our lives, our understanding of the world changed. And there is no going back to our old ways. We have been touched by the overpowering perfume of God's love and grace— an amazing gift.

* * *

Questions for Contemplation or Discussion

1. In many ways Mary was acting in a way that was counter-culture. She listened to a rabbi, she sat at his feet, she touched his feet—at very daring act—and she let down her hair in public. What does this say about her?

2. She was misunderstood. Have you ever had your motives or actions misunderstood? How did you deal with it?

3. In what ways do you think women of faith are living a counter-culture life to-day?

Salome

A Follower of Jesus

Matthew 20: 20-23; 27:55-56

Background

We know that Salome was the wife of the fisherman Zebedee and the mother of James and John. At the crucifixion she is mentioned by name in some Gospels and in others there is reference to Mary's sister. There are some interpreters who understand Salome to be this sister of Mary, the mother of Jesus. While this cannot be proven it makes the story of James and John very interesting. They would be Jesus' cousins, and Salome his aunt if one takes this position.

* * *

Sometimes it is very hard to look back on one's life and sees one's errors. As I sit here, an old woman reflecting on my life, it brings both great joy and deep sadness.

I knew of my nephew Jesus and had heard from Mary the story of his birth and knew him as a child. My boys, James and John, played with him when they were young. And I will never forget the time Jesus got left behind in the temple. Mary assumed he was with us and we expected he was with his parents. What a fright it was for all of us. But all's well that ends well. However, Mary and I felt that he was never going to be an ordinary carpenter.

As young men, their lives took different paths. Jesus became a carpenter and worked in his boyhood town of Nazareth. My boys followed their father into the fishing business and worked on Lake Galilee. We saw less of each other.

But one year at Passover we met again in Jerusalem. Our sons were grown men now, around thirty years of age. They spent some time together talking and then each returned to their own life.

Not long after that, Jesus showed up at our boat. He called to my sons and invited them to join him and become fishers of men. With our blessing they went away with Jesus and became his disciples. There were ten others who were a part of those who followed Jesus. I too was one who believed that he was the one to free us from Roman tyranny.

Jesus was gathering large crowds of people who followed him and listened to his every word. He spoke often of the coming of the kingdom of God. My sons were part of the three followers who were closest to Jesus. Peter was the other one. He was a big brash man, who often spoke before he thought.

I felt that when Jesus established his kingdom he would need good men to help him rule. I thought

Peter just wasn't the right person. He was a good man and a sincere follower of Jesus, but he didn't have what it takes to be a leader over the people of this land. Jesus needed close advisers who knew him well and could assist him in his reign. There came a day when I felt the time was right to ask a favour of him.

And so I went to my nephew and asked that when he declared his kingdom, he give careful consideration to making his cousins, his right and left hand men. They were in his inner circle now and it seemed proper that they continue to be his closest advisors.

Well! He put me in my place. He said it was God who would make that choice not him.

Looking back I see how far off the mark I was. I simply did not understand him or his mission or purpose. Nor did I understand that he was not planning a political kingdom, but a spiritual one.

But he was truly a man of God and he never held any bitterness at my ambition for my sons or me.

At his death, as I stood there at the cross, I finally understood. It was so bitterly painful to see how wrong I had been. And now, we are coming to know him in a new and different light. He is still our rabbi, but present in a different way. Still leading us, teaching us and guiding us, but in spirit now, not as the nephew I loved. He is now the Christ, the anointed one, the deliverer. Thanks be to God.

* * *

Questions for Contemplation or Discussion.

1.   Have you heard this interpretation of the relationship between Mary and Salome before? Does it change anything in the story for you?

2.   What things might a mother learn from this story?

3.   Matthew only identifies her by her role, never her name. Have you ever been identified solely by your role? As a daughter, wife, mother? If so, how does it make you feel?

Chapter 6
Women Near the Cross

Faithful to the End

In this chapter we hear from women who are a part of the crucifixion narrative. Johanna, Mary the mother of Jesus, Mary who lived in Jerusalem, Mary of Magdala are all mentioned in the gospels. Mary of Magdala, often called Mary Magdalene, is present in all four gospels, Matthew, Mark, Luke and John. Her place in the story is so important that all four stories mention her by name.

Claudia, the wife of Pilate is part of the story of the trial of Jesus but she is not named by Matthew. Her name comes from secular history. Judas' mother is there because he must have had a mother and I have often wondered how she dealt with her son's death. The monologue telling her story comes from that curiosity.

The story of Mary of Magdala is a very rich one. Over the years I have told her story from a number of perspectives. One is my story of her life before she met Jesus, another as she was one of the women disciples and of course, at Easter. The same is true for Sarah. I have told her story in many ways from different times in her life and experience. At one time at Easter I used eight women to enrich the story for us in our times. The six named above and the other two were the unnamed girl by the fire, and one of the women in the crowd along the streets where Jesus carried his cross.

These women near the cross were women who were close to Jesus and were with him as he healed the sick and taught the crowds. They stayed at the scene and watched him suffer and die. These women were strong and faithful and lived in ways that make them role models even these many centuries later.

To read their stories is to reach back to the pre-Christian era and touch the roots of this world encompassing faith

Mary
Of Jerusalem
Mark 14: 51, Acts 12: 11-17

Background

There is a tradition which states that this Mary was the mother of John Mark and the last supper was held at her home. While scholars do not all agree, a reasonable case can be made for this. Many believe that John Mark wrote the gospel of Mark. We know that his mother's name was Mary. In this gospel there is one verse that states that a young man was witness to the scene in the garden and when confronted left his cloak and ran away. If Mary's house was the scene of the last supper, then this young man, her son, could have overheard the disciples and Jesus and followed them to the garden.

* * *

After the disciples left my home, my friends and I began to clean up after their long and somewhat mysterious dinner and conversation. We women came and went from the room where they were gathered, and so I heard some of the conversation. It was very puzzling and disturbing. There was the talk about the bread and wine and the body and blood of Jesus. I didn't understand that at all. Very strange. And then Judas left early, and he seemed to be disturbed about

145

something. But Judas was often different from the rest of them. I hope that Jesus will explain it all to us tomorrow.

We were almost finished cleaning up when I noticed that I hadn't seen my son, John Mark. He needed to fill the heavy water jars for me. He always did that, usually without being asked. I looked around for him, called to him, but he was not in the house. I wondered where he was, but he was a sensible boy and I was confident he would return soon.

After the other women had left, I sat down to rest and I must have fallen asleep. For I was suddenly aware that someone had burst into the room. It was John Mark. He looked frightened, he was breathing hard and sweating, as if he had been running, and his cloak was missing. His knees and elbows were skinned, so he must have fallen in his hurry. He was talking so fast I couldn't really understand him, as he was sobbing at the same time.

I persuaded him to sit and brought him water to wash his face, hoping that would calm him. I could make out a few words: Jesus praying in the garden, Roman soldiers, Judas, traitor, Jesus arrested and taken away, Peter fighting with his sword, but it wasn't very easy to understand. He was so out of breath, crying and trembling. He seemed very frightened.

I finally got him into bed and with a little watered wine, and some gentle talking and singing, I got him to go to sleep. But he was still restless, thrashing about, and crying out, "No, no, not Jesus."

John Mark has always been a thoughtful child, taking everything in and trying to understand adult things. He took his studies at the rabbi's school very seriously. I couldn't understand all the ideas that he talked about, and I wished that his father was still here to talk about it with him. It is hard to raise a boy alone, and sometimes I think I have not been a very wise mother to this quick, intelligent son of mine.

He was so caught up in the coming of the Messiah, that I worried he would get involved with some of the groups that were agitating and planning to try and over throw the Roman rulers who now governed our land. I was so pleased when he began to spend time with Jesus and his followers. I felt he could come to no harm when he was with such a gentle and kind teacher. His words were always about love and mercy and God's grace. I didn't think my boy could come to any harm with Jesus and his disciples. But perhaps I was wrong.

I think I'll just sleep here beside his bed in case he wakes and needs me. The morning brings light to our world, and I am sure it will bring some light and understanding to the events of this night. John Mark will make more sense in the morning and one of the disciples or Jesus will be able to explain it all. But now I must rest, for tomorrow will bring its own troubles, and I am very weary.

* * *

Questions for Contemplation or Discussion

1. What is your feeling about this interpretation of Mary and her son John Mark's place in the crucifixion story?

2. From other stories we know that Mary's home was a centre for the Christian faith in the early years. (Acts 12:12) What might her role have been?

3. John Mark became a missionary traveling with Paul. What do you think prepared him for this task?

Johanna
Wife of Chuza
Luke 8:1-3; 24:10

Background

Scripture tells us that Joanna was married to Chuza, a steward in the house of Herod. He oversaw the running of the estate and was an influential man in the palace. As his wife, Joanna would have been respected and would have enjoyed some freedom as an important woman. She was understood and accepted by Jesus and became one of his followers.

* * *

My life in the household of Herod was one of ease and comfort. I lacked for nothing in the ways of life's material goods. Exotic foods were served at every meal, my clothing was the finest that could be purchased, and my living quarters were elegant and comfortable. I should have been a very happy woman —but I was not.

I was a Jew but I was not welcomed in the homes of Jewish women. They were always concerned that I might be a spy for Herod and were distant and reserved around me. I was never invited into their homes and whenever we went to worship, we were again not welcome and left completely alone. At the palace, because I was a Jew, I was once again under suspicion. The circles of friendship among the Romans were closed to me. That was enough of a burden but I was also feeling ill, heart sick I think, much of the time.

I heard of the teacher and healer Jesus, and at some risk to myself and my husband, I sought him out. Just a smile, a touch of his hand, and a few words of acceptance and I was completely well.

I began to go where he was, and to listen to him. Before long I was a part of the circle of women who followed him and cared for him in many ways. It was a wonderful experience for me.

I was totally accepted. No questions asked. No suspicious glances. The conversation never stopped because I was near. In fact, I was invited to join the group of women and to share their lives completely. We talked together, talked of all the things that women talk about: clothes, hair, food, homes and children. But we also talked about the teachings of Jesus. We were included in the talks that Jesus had with his male followers. There was no setting us apart because we were women. We were his followers too and he treated us all as equals. It was such a joy and a delight to belong to a community. And what a wonderful community. Loving and caring, welcoming and open, a place for me to learn, to share and to belong.

And then it all came crashing down. Jesus, arrested, tried, sentenced and crucified. Had anyone said this was to happen, I never would have believed it, but I have seen it with my own eyes. I heard the rabble calling for him to be killed. I saw Pilot wash his hands, as he let Jesus be taken away. He watched this gentle man be spat on, slapped, crowned with thorns, and then dragged out to be killed.

I had to leave. I could not bear to stay. But some did. His mother, and Mary, and maybe some of the others. I was too crushed. Too heartbroken. Too afraid of the future. How could we carry on now that he was gone? His followers, his teachings, his love, were what I lived for each and every day. What will become of all of us?

He was buried quickly in a borrowed tomb. Joseph of Arimithea said they could use his tomb and they took him away quickly because of the Sabbath.

When we can move about again, when Sabbath is ended, we women are going to the tomb to anoint his body. There was no time to prepare him properly. I have ointments and spices, and I will take them and meet the others to do what needs to be done for the one who meant everything to me.

I don't know how I will be able to do it, but I will not be alone. We women will draw strength from each other, and we will do this last service to our teacher and our friend. It is all that we can do.

* * *

Questions for Contemplation or Discussion

1. Women stayed at the cross until the very end of Jesus' life. Can you speculate on how or why they did this while the male disciples all went away?

2. These women were with Jesus daily. How do you make room for the presence of the holy in your daily routine?

3. Why is this important to you?

Mary
Of Magdala

John 19: 25b, 20: 1-18

Background

For years Mary of Magdala, often called Mary Magdalene, has been portrayed as a prostitute. There is nothing in scripture to affirm this idea. She was healed by Jesus of infirmities and evil spirits. Today we might name her bipolar or another ailment, but she was a sick woman, not a prostitute. Jesus healed her and she became a faithful follower.

* * *

How well I remember that night. After seeing his broken body hanging on the cross, then quickly placed in a tomb, we women left to go to our homes. We were a broken-hearted group. Our hopes for the future had ended hanging on those ugly wooden poles. All the joy and peace I had come to know as a normal life were sucked out of me as I watched him die.

Before we women parted, we agreed that we would meet early on the morning after the Sabbath ended and we would go together to anoint his body for

153

burial. It was all that we could do for him now, and it was something we needed to do.

I waited. Hardly sleeping. Barely eating. For three days I sat and remembered—remembered the wonderful feeling that I experienced after he healed me. No longer was I bound by an illness I could not control. Our physicians could do nothing for me. They said I was possessed and should be put away, segregated from the rest of the world. How fortunate for me, that I was a woman of means and could pay the bribes needed to keep my freedom. When I felt an attack coming, I simply shut myself in my house until it passed. My imprisonment was of my own doing and was not permanent.

All this ended when I met Jesus. To be one of his followers gave my life meaning and purpose. I had friends. I was respected and treated as simply one of the women who helped to care for Jesus. We aided his ministry in many ways. Cooking, sewing, treating minor illnesses, and of course, we supported his followers with our money, those of us who had the means to do that.

Early on the morning after Sabbath, I got ready. Dressed warmly, I gathered up the burial cloths that I had prepared. I met the other women at the gate to the garden, and we paused together for a moment. A moment of grief to offer support and comfort to each other.

Quietly, reverently, we made our way to the tomb. Salome wondered aloud how we could roll the stone away. We looked at each other and stood still. As we stood there, perplexed, the ground shook, the trees trembled and the air was filled with noise, like a rushing wind. Shaken and afraid, we wondered what to do. Johanna said, "I've come this far, I'm not running away now." We took courage from her words and walked toward the tomb.

Johanna was a little ahead when we saw her stop and then heard her gasp.

She turned and said," The stone has been moved." Quickly we went to the gaping hole in the side of the hill. Stopping at the doorway, we saw the tomb was empty. Stunned, we stood for a moment. A strange light filled the space and I heard a voice. And I knew that they should go and find Peter and the rest of the disciples and tell them what we had found.

Quickly they turned and walked, almost ran, back out of the garden to find Peter. I stood by the tomb in shock. What had happened here? What did the earthquake mean? Where was the body? And how to explain the beautiful light and the voice?

I saw a figure in the shadows and went to him. I thought he was someone who tended the garden and so I went and asked if he knew where the body was. He turned slowly to face me, and quietly said, "Mary."

At once I recognized his voice. It was my

friend, my healer, my teacher. I called out, "Rabboni, teacher." He moved a little away and said that I should not touch him, but should go and tell the disciples. I could hardly believe my eyes. It wasn't over. He was still with us. His peace once again filled my heart and I knew that I would never feel alone again.

*   *   *

Questions for Discussion or Contemplation

1. The gospels tell the crucifixion and resurrection story with many differing details. How do you account for this? Does it affect your response to the story?

2. Mary of Magdala plays a very important role in the Easter story. All the gospels name her as being present. Why do you think she is recognized by all the writers?

3. What meaning does resurrection have for you in your life to-day?

Delora
Mother of Judas
Matthew 27: 3-5

Background

There is nothing in scripture concerning Judas' mother. To separate him from human connections, helps to dehumanize Judas and make him someone with whom we cannot or do not identify. To think about his mother and what the events of this time meant to her, makes the story one that we might identify with in some ways.

* * *

My name, Delora, means sorrow. I never liked my name for I was a happy child, full of laughter and joy. I wanted to change it, but mother said that it was the right name for me. How right she was.

My son Judas was a strange little boy. He was always very serious. As a child he was never carefree and he always feared the worst. Most of his days were spent alone, in quiet sombre play, if you can call what he did play. He seemed angry all of the time, and was sullen and withdrawn. As a youth, his anger became focused on the conditions we lived in. The sight of

Roman legions made him furious and I worried he would do something foolish. I know he had acquaintances in the Sicarii. It means dagger men and they are dedicated to violence to drive out the Romans. I was afraid he would join them and that his life would be at risk.

You can imagine my joy when he joined the band of disciples that were going around the countryside with the rabbi Jesus. Jesus taught love and peace and forgiveness and mercy. Such a contrast to the hate filled words of the Sicarii.

I went to the hillside to hear him for myself. I found a man who was kind, gentle and full of the wisdom of our ancestors. He spoke of the God who blessed people, not cursed or punished them. He spoke of loving our neighbours, of walking a second mile in kindness and mercy. He gave hope to the hopeless, comfort to the sorrowing, and healing to those who were suffering.

It seemed to me that he was goodness itself in human form. I was so happy that Judas was in his presence. I felt he must grow more at peace within himself and also with the world around him.

Judas seemed more content in those days and I began to hope that he had a positive future with Jesus. He followed him to the lakeside villages and spent time listening to his teachings.

I was very pleased when I learned they had given Judas the responsibility of keeping their meager funds, and paying for their needs. I felt it showed that they trusted him and he really belonged with them.

However, sometimes I worried, for he spoke once of a woman who had anointed Jesus, wasting a lot of money as she poured out her oil on his head and feet. I saw a flash of his old anger as he called out in a harsh voice what should be done with her. But it didn't last and I held on to my hopes and dreams for my son.

Then I heard the terrible news. Jesus had been arrested and taken away to be crucified. I prayed that Judas was safe and that somehow he had not been a part of that ugly scene. I hoped he and the other disciples were far away from it all and safe. But I wondered what kind of a world I lived in, where a kind and gentle teacher could be arrested and taken away.

Many hours later they came to me with my son's body. They said something about him throwing money at the priests and the elders, then running away crying out like a wounded animal. The men who brought Judas to me, said that they knew nothing else, and that his body had been found by some people walking through the valley. They mentioned that the authorities were searching for his followers, and asked me what I knew. I could honestly tell them I knew nothing.

All my hopes were dashed. All of it had come

to nothing. Jesus was dead. His disciples scattered and hiding. How I wished Judas was with them. But Judas has never run away. Not from bullies who made his boyhood miserable. Not from soldiers when he got in their way and they tried to arrest him. And not from whatever had recently troubled him.

He would choose to end his life rather than admit he was wrong, or disappointed, or had failed in some way. So now he is dead. My baby. My little boy. My unhappy child and my grown son.

What a night. Two men have died horrible deaths and for what? Whatever Jesus was trying to do has failed, and his failure has cost me my only son. How will I carry on? What hope is there for me? What hope is there for this world?

I remember that Jesus had some women followers along with the men. I wonder where they are. Tomorrow I shall look for them. They will know. Women are wise and they can help me to understand. Tomorrow I will find some peace in spite of all this tragedy, with the women who followed Jesus.

* * *

Questions for Discussion or Contemplation

1. What do you think of this imaginative story? Do you think this is a fair telling of her story?

2. If you agree, what would you add? If not how would you portray this woman?

3. How do women assist each other in times of grief and pain?

Mary
Wife of Clopas

John 19:25   Luke 24: 13-35

Background

There are a number of theories regarding Clopas/Cleopas among scholars. There is also discussion as to who the other Mary was who was at the crucifixion. It is thought by some that this Mary was the wife of Clopas who lived in the village of Emmaus. If so, she was the mother of James and Joseph or Joses. If we take these theories as a starting point for a story about her, does it not seem logical that she was going home, walking with her husband on the road to Emmaus?

* * *

As I sit in my garden and reflect on my life, what wonderful things I have seen.

I was raised as any young Galilean girl and taught all the skills I needed to be a wife and a mother: cooking, weaving, sewing, mending, and cleaning. But unlike many girls, I was taught to think for myself as well. We were Jews, and I watched my mother light the Sabbath candles for our supper meal. I often

163

wondered how she could find such joy in that simple task. At times I was sure she was so tired she could hardly stand with all the work that was needed for the Sabbath supper, but it always brought a light to her eyes that I never saw at any other time.

She told me that I too would find great pleasure in our Sabbath rituals when I had my own home. And she was absolutely right. There was always a sense of joy and hope as I prepared the meal and lit the candles. I was happy being a wife and mother and following the old ways.

But my sons led me in a new direction. They were followers of the new Rabbi, the one they called Jesus. I listened to them talk of their leader and he seemed so different. My sons spoke of women who traveled with him and of the way Jesus taught them, listened to them, and treated them as friends and partners.

I heard how he healed the sick and cured the lame, made the blind see and touched the lepers, healing them and making them whole again. I also heard how he welcomed children to him, holding them on his lap, smiling and laughing with them, and giving them his blessing. I thought that I would like to know someone like him.

And so I went with my sons to hear and to see for myself. It was a new day for me. And at once I became a follower and brought my husband Clopas to hear Jesus too. It was wonderful that the whole family was sharing in this new message of peace and hope.

And then it all came crashing down around us. Clopas and I were in Jerusalem for the Passover, for we still kept many of our Jewish feasts.

I was there on that hill to watch him die. When John took his mother away from that awful scene, I left as well. I returned to the small room at the inn and waited for news. We did not know where our sons were and we were afraid for them. We stayed there until we could travel to Emmaus, it being the Sabbath day. But we left just as soon as we could without attracting any attention

On the road, we were very sad, frightened and full of despair. Suddenly, we were joined by a stranger. We began to talk and told him of our great loss. He asked some questions and then talked to us about the prophets and the hope that they taught. We walked and talked until we were at our home. We invited him in, as it was not safe for a person to travel alone after dark.

I prepared a simple meal and we gathered to eat. He took the bread and broke it and shared it amongst us. Somehow at that moment we knew. We knew beyond any doubt that it was our rabbi. And then he was gone.

Danger or not, we just left everything and almost ran back to Jerusalem. We went to the house of Mary where we had been for the evening that Jesus was arrested and we found all our friends there. Mary said that she had seen Jesus and talked to him. Peter and John would only say that the grave was empty and there was no body. Thomas was full of doubt and kept saying we were having delusions.

But Clopas and I were able to tell them of our experience and I guess there was something about our faces as we told it, that they began to believe us and Mary.

We never saw him again, but we knew that in some new and wonderful way he was with us, each and every day. My sons went about telling the story and teaching anyone who would listen.

Clopas and I continued to live in Emmaus till he died and now I am here alone, waiting for my time to die. What lies ahead I don't know. But I do know that the rabbi told us he was going to prepare a place for us, and someday, we would be together with our loved ones and with him. I am content and I trust the Holy One for whatever tomorrow will bring.

* * *

Questions for Contemplation or Discussion

1. Why do you think they did not recognize Jesus?

2. Why would they suddenly recognize him at the table?

3. What would it mean for us to take a walk along the Emmaus road?

Claudia
Wife of Pilot
Matthew 27: 15-26

Background

Pilate as procurator of Judea was the only one who had the authority to pronounce a sentence of death. When Jesus was before him and on trial, his wife, Claudia, sent him a note in support of Jesus. She was descended from a Patrician Roman and would have grown up in the halls of power.

* * *

What strange twists and turns my life has taken. Raised in the highest circles in Rome, I was used to the best of everything. I lived in palaces and ate the food of the gods. My life was filled with parties and wonderful gowns and everything that money could buy.

When I married Pontius Pilate, I expected that kind of life would continue. I would move to a different palace, but nothing else would change. Pilate was a good husband to me: caring, kind and affectionate. He did everything to please me. I was happy and expected my life to continue as it had always been.

But no! For some reason Pilate was sent to Judea and here is where I have lived. In this hot dry, dusty back water of the world. It seemed to be a very strange country, with an even stranger people living in it. They worshipped only one god, not many, as I was used to. This god seemed to be one who had a lot of rules, including one about making images. Very strange and unreasonable.

Every time Pilot tried to improve the country, to make its plain buildings beautiful, he was opposed by these Jews. They rioted over a few shields hung to grace their dingy place of worship. They were so angry he had to remove them, or wage a very costly war.

I was determined to learn more about these people and what they believed. I learned of a rabbi who was drawing great crowds. He was said to be a great teacher and healer. I dressed in my simplest clothes and wore a plain cape and covered my hair and face with a hood.

I found him nearby surrounded by a great crowd of people. They were dressed like peasants and smelled like sheep and fish. I could barely stand it, but I stayed on the edges and listened to what he had to say. His words were such as I had never heard before. He spoke of kindness, mercy, love and justice. His voice was quiet and yet held such power that I could not leave. I went many times to hear him and each time I was drawn in by his gentleness.

Pilate was not well; something was bothering him. He tossed and turned all night, at times crying out in his dreams. I knew that Jesus was heading for trouble with the authorities and expected that Pilate was being drawn into the struggle. How I wished that encounter could be avoided. If Pilate stood against Jesus, he would once more anger the people.

He was very late coming home one day, and I learned from the servants that he was overseeing a trial of someone accused of wanting to be king. The way they spoke of the prisoner, I knew it was Jesus. I tried to rest, and when I fell asleep I had a dream. The dream told me that this trial meant trouble for us no matter what Pilate decreed. I remembered Jesus' words, and I knew that he had no desire to be a king in a palace. I did not understand what he was hoping for, but I knew that it was not going to espouse anything that could be considered a crime against Rome.

I called a trusted servant and told him to go to Pilate. "Tell my husband that I have had a dream, and that he should have nothing to do with this man. Let him go. He does not deserve punishment." I went to the hall to listen. I hid behind one of the pillars. I heard Pilate say that he found no fault in Jesus and I could see he had heeded my message. He tried to have him released and another criminal stand in his place, but the rabble would not agree. Pilate turned Jesus over to them and symbolically washed his hands. He was hoping that he could forget what he had done, and bear no guilt. It makes me tremble even now, even though it happened so long ago.

But I knew it was the beginning of the end for us. Whatever happened, history would not forget. I would not forget and Pilate would not forget.

It has been years since that day and it still haunts us both. I think the end of our time is near. Some things cannot be easily forgotten and we must bear the scars for the rest of our lives. The throngs that followed Jesus have become a strong yet gentle force for good in our land and I think that day was a turning point in our lives. I am ready for whatever comes. The talk is that as he died Jesus forgave everyone who had been a part of his dying. Can their God really be that merciful? I hope and pray that it is so.

* * *

Questions for Contemplation or Discussion

1. Do you think Pilate listened to the warning from Claudia? If so, why do you think he did not do more to save Jesus? If he paid her no heed then why did he not condemn him to death?

2. Because of her dream, Claudia tried to intervene in the trial. Once again Jesus revealed

172

himself to a woman and a foreigner. What thoughts do you have about this pattern in Jesus' life?

3. To-day, are women prophets and preachers heard if their message differs from the traditional message of the church?

Mary
Mother of the Crucified Jesus
John 19: 25b-27

Background

What we know of Mary is gleaned from a few verses as the Gospel writers tell the story of Jesus and his ministry. The information about his mother was not important to the writers, but she was a woman, with all the emotions of a human mother. She must have been puzzled, worried, hopeful, and afraid for the future of the child she loved and cared for.

* * *

So many years ago, the angel had said to me, "Do not be afraid." But I had been afraid, so many times. It began with the visit from the angel, then at his birth, and the time when he stayed behind in Jerusalem at the temple, and later when the crowds turned ugly and wanted to stone him. And now it has come to this horrible end.

I knew that I had a very important and special task in raising this child. I watched over him day and night, tending to his every need. Every time he skinned his knees when he played in the village, I felt that I had failed in my task. Whenever he cried in pain, or fear, or loneliness, I wept with him, both for him and for my shortcomings as his mother. I taught him the ways of our people, sent him to be trained by the rabbis, heard his lisping prayers, and watched as he seemed to live in his own world. In many ways he seemed to be wiser than any of us. He would get that far away look in his eye, and seem to be listening to a voice that only he could hear. But this! Who could have imagined this!

Just a few hours ago, I saw him hanging on an ugly cross on a hill. Crucified between two thieves. Treated like a common criminal. To stand there and watch him suffer was more than I could bear. No mother should have to watch something like that. Finally, at Jesus' request, John took me away and took me to his home.

There I was given food and drink, though I wanted neither. I was given warm water in which to bathe and a comfortable mat on which I could rest. I sat on a stool and tried to understand.

The words of Isaiah rushed into my head and pounded in my ears. He has borne our afflictions, a man of suffering and grief, despised and rejected, led to the slaughter, silent like a beast. They told me that the temple veil was torn from top to bottom. I suppose that means something, but is that what God does when we suffer? Is that God's answer to my pain and my grief?

Where is the liberty and justice that the prophets foretold? Where is the God of love and mercy that Jesus spoke about? Where is the peace that the rabbis say is our birthright as God's people? It seems to be out there bleeding and dying on that hill.

I hope that someone will bury him; will find a tomb where he can rest for eternity. He can't be left out there on that garbage dump. Surely someone will care for him. Where are his disciples? Those brave strong men ran away in fear. When I left, the women were still there. Women know what to do. They will take care of him. They loved him too, just as I did.

I think back to old Anna in the temple. She had tears on her cheeks when she looked at me and the child. She knew the Holy Words, having been in the temple for so many years listening. What did she see? Could she have foreseen this ending to his life?

But we have been taught that God is merciful and loving. I wonder can this really be the end? What did David say in his psalm?

> O Lord my God, I cried to you for help, and you
> have healed me.
> You restored me to life from among those who
> go down to the pit.
> Sing praises to the Lord, O you his saints, and
> give thanks to his holy name.
> For his anger is but for a moment and his favor
> is for a lifetime.

Weeping may tarry for the night, but joy comes
with the morning.
(Psalm 30. Selected Verses RSV)
I will sleep now, waiting for the joy which
comes in the morning. It has to come or how can I go
on living?

* * *

Questions for Contemplation or Discussion

1. The church has put Mary on a pedestal. Do
you see her as the Queen of Heaven or as a simple
peasant woman? Or both?
2. How do you feel about the way this story
portrays Mary?
3, What does it mean to have joy in the morning
during times of grief or sadness? Have you ever sensed
this in your life?

Chapter 7
Women in the Early Church

Learning About Them

Women were the last disciples at the cross and the first at the empty tomb. They were active and valued for the work they did in the church in its early years. We know a great deal about the church fathers, but are only now beginning to find the lost stories of the church mothers.

Of the six women I name, five of them were closely connected to Paul. The sixth was known and loved by Peter. Paul had a reputation for keeping women in silent, passive roles in the church, but there is ample evidence that women worked with Paul and he respected and honoured their gifts.

A number of women served as leaders of the house churches that sprang up in the cities of the Roman Empire. The list includes: Priscilla, Chloe, Lydia, Apphia, Nympha and the mother of John Mark. Each one of these women is named by Paul in his letters.

The study of how this inclusion of women was reversed is too long and complex to explore here, however, we need to remember that women were definitely among Jesus' closest followers and leaders in the early years of the Christian faith. They have always carved out a place for themselves and carried the teachings of Jesus into each century, in spite of those who felt they were lesser beings than men.

These stories may pique your interest in our foremothers and their role in the church of past centuries and the church of today. If it does, there is a wealth of information on line and in published books and articles.

Celebrate the role and place of women in the spiritual lives of humankind through all the generations, including our own.

Damaris

Acts 17: 22-34

Background

Athens was an intellectual centre and Paul was expanding his territory for spreading the gospel. He was disturbed by all the idols and began speaking in the market place. Greek women had some freedom. They could own property and received some education. Wealthy Greek women were able to continue their learning and women of the upper classes also had more freedom of movement.

* * *

As a Greek woman of means and status, my life was pleasant and interesting. My father saw that I was educated. I could read and write; I had studied literature, read the great authors, attended the theatre and often listened to the political and judicial debates.

With slaves and servants to do the menial work at our home, I was free to pursue my interests. Dionysius was a member of the council. He was one of the ruling judges in the city. We were good friends and enjoyed stimulating discussions. The court cases of a serious nature were held at the Areopagus, a rocky knoll of marble, near the Acropolis. When the trials were being held, I often wrapped myself in an old cloak and stood in the shadows nearby to listen. I found the discussions and arguments very interesting and the next day I would discuss it all with Dionysius.

On one of these days, he said that he had heard a most interesting speech by a man at the market. This man, Paul, was a Jew with Roman citizenship. That alone made him a curiosity. Dionysius said his talk was about a Jewish Rabbi who had been put to death as a criminal. According to Paul there was little evidence to convict him, but mobs are difficult to reason with. It was rumoured that Paul was going to speak from the Areopagus and some of the judges, rulers and priests were going to hear him. I was intrigued by all this and decided that I would be there too.

I arrived early and was able to get a place near enough to be able to see and hear this man who was causing such interest. When he arrived and climbed to the top of the hill, I was very surprised. He was not at all as I had expected.

He certainly didn't look Roman at all. Wearing the dusty robes of a traveller, sandals and cloak of no particular colour, he was a very undistinguished figure. He was short, and completely bald. His legs were bowed out and yet they were sturdy and well-muscled. He was well built, and perhaps had done some training in the Roman gymnasiums. His face was small, not attractive at all, with eye-brows that met over a very long nose. But I noticed he walked with a dignity and grace that was more commonly seen among the aristocrats than the peasant he appeared to be. I had no idea what to expect and waited with much interest and some excitement.

He began with proper formality. "Citizens of Athens," he said a strong, clear voice. He then spoke of all our beautiful statues and said he noticed how particular we were in the matters of religion. I was pleased with his words. He showed that he was man who respected the gifts and artistry of our people, and he recognized our religion and our gods. To this point I saw nothing unusual about him, except his appearance.

He then said, "I see you have an altar dedicated 'to an Unknown God.' I am here to tell you about that God." He then began to speak of a prophet, a rabbi, a healer and a teacher named Jesus. He talked for a very long time, but it passed as if it was a moment. I was fascinated, intrigued and wanted to know more about this God who was the creator and father of all of us.

We followed him and talked further. We, Dionysius, Paul and I met a number of times. By the time he left us, we were both convinced of the truth of his message.

We became believers.

* * *

Questions for Contemplation or Discussion

1.   It doesn't seem as if there was a church in Athens. What do you suppose happened after Paul left?

2.   As an educated and prominent woman might she have begun a church in her home? What makes you come to your conclusion?

3.   How important is it to have a community in which to worship?

Eunice

Acts 16:1-3, 2
Timothy 1:5

Background

Eunice and her mother lived together in Lystra. They were Jews and kept the Jewish faith. Eunice married a Greek, but there is no mention of him other than that fact. It is likely that he had died previously. Paul made at least two trips to Lystra to spread the story of Jesus as the Messiah.

* * *

My mother, Lois, raised me in the faith of our forefathers and mothers. It was her task to teach me to be a good Jewish wife and mother. I learned to cook our meals according to our laws about food. It was complicated and I sometimes forgot or got confused, but mother was a patient teacher. She taught me the rules about mixing two kinds of cloth. That rule was simple, it was forbidden. As I grew older she taught me the rituals about Sabbath, and that the mother was the teacher in the family. and the one who held them close to our faith.

When I came of age to marry I was married to a Greek man, who knew not our God nor our history.

He was a good man, kind and understanding. He never forbade us to practise our rituals, and he never questioned or denigrated our customs. They must have seemed strange to him, but he just observed and kept his silence.

When our son was born, I gave him a Jewish name. Lystra was a city of many races and just as many religions, and many, many gods. I wanted Timothy to learn the ways of our people. His name meant, one who fears God, and I worked hard to help that become true for my son.

Mother was a wonderful teacher. Timothy loved her and he listened to her and obeyed her without question. There was a wonderful bond between them, and I was so happy for them both. He was schooled by the rabbi and took his studies very seriously.

When he was a young man, two men—Paul and Barnabas—came to our city. They came to teach about a man they said was the Messiah, and for whom we had been waiting for so many centuries. As they told us about him, we three became believers in this new faith. It was a gentle way of life, for the teachings were about peace, love, mercy and the joy that this way of following God brought. It touched our hearts and we three became Christians.

While he was teaching in the city, the crowd turned against them and tried to stone Paul. He survived, and when he was able, left the city and travelled to other places to spread the story of Jesus. We continued to gather with other believers and to help Timothy learn the ways of Jesus, the Christ.

Some years later, Paul returned. Timothy was fascinated that in spite of the way he was treated he returned to continue teaching in the city. Paul spent a great deal of time with Timothy and he often told us that we had raised a fine young man. He stated the words of Solomon. "She who bore you shall rejoice," and said to us that we should rejoice because we had raised a good man.

I might not have been as pleased as I was, if I had known what Paul had in mind. Paul wanted Timothy to go with him and to be his companion in his ministry. The first obstacle was that Timothy's father was neutral about most of our practices, but he forbade me to have him circumcised. Paul said it was necessary, as they would be preaching to Jews as they travelled and this sign of faithfulness was necessary if Timothy was to have any credibility.

We agreed, and I was actually very happy about it. Now my son was a member of the covenant, a son of Abraham. Mother and I nursed him until he was healed and then we prepared to let him go with Paul.

It is hard to watch your son go away with such a powerful man. I had many doubts. Would they try again to stone him, and would Timothy be in danger? What about shipwrecks? Wars? Diseases? Who would look after him? Who would see that he ate properly, wash his clothes, bind his wounds? Would I ever see him again?

But mother reminded me that he was a man. A man called by God to go and tell others what he had learned. Trying not to show my fear, I said good-bye and if I held him a little too tightly and for a little too long, he would just have to understand.

"Go with God, my son. Go with God."

* * *

Questions for Contemplation or Discussion

1. Knowing that Paul was almost killed for his beliefs, what do you think drew these women into the new faith that he was teaching?

2. In your experience, is it women who teach the faith to the next generation?

3. These women were behind the scenes to some degree. Do you know of women who live their lives in the shadow of someone?

Priscilla

Acts 18:1-3, 18-19, 24-28

Background

Priscilla and her husband Aquila were converts to the Christian faith and, friends and co-workers of Paul. From the text she is clearly addressed as an equal to her husband and they were partners in a house ministry.

* * *

As I sit here at my spinning I think back on my life. Spinning the yarn takes no concentration and so my mind is free to wander.

I remember my childhood and youth. Born into a noble family, life was pleasant and very comfortable. My family were of Latin descent but were Jews by birth, and followers of the Rabbi Jesus, by choice. Because we lived as all Jews do, observant of the laws of God, we had a good life. It was a way of life that not only brought God's peace, but the rules of our diet, meant that we were healthy, when many of the people of Rome were often ill with various ailments.

I met and married Aquila who also was a convert from Judaism. He was a good man, a tentmaker, who worked with leather as his main trade.

He was a hard worker. His goods were of excellent quality and so my life changed little when I married. I worked alongside him in the trade and I also kept the books and saw that everything was organized.

We were expelled from Rome by the Emperor Claudius. We Jews were often on the move for any number of reasons, and expulsion from a town or country was not unusual.

We went to Corinth and settled with the small Jewish community that was there. We began to worship in our home and one day the missionary Paul came to our city. Since we were all in the same trade, he stayed with us for many months. The church grew and prospered and I was very happy in this home. But it didn't last.

Paul was going to Ephesus to spread the message that Jesus taught and invited us to go with him and start a house church there. The one in Corinth was strong and we knew it would carry on without us.

Paul stayed for some time as we worked together to build a basis for the Christian faith in that very corrupt and licentious city. They needed to hear the message of love, compassion and hope that the Christian story brought. Paul left and we were now the leaders of this new church.

It became a thriving place of worship, teaching and prayer, and we decided to move again and to go to

Ephesus. It was a centre of religion and philosophy, but the people worshipped many gods and goddesses. Once again our words about Jesus and his teachings touched the people's hearts and our house churches began to grow. Not just in numbers but in understanding.

There was a man, a Jew named Apollos, who was teaching about Jesus in the synagogue. He was a good teacher, but he didn't have the whole story of Jesus' life and teachings. I invited him to dinner, and spent many hours with him, telling him about Jesus and teaching him The Way, which is what we called our new faith.

We were completely devastated to hear that Paul had been executed. Such a special man, a wonderful missionary for the new faith, and a good and dear friend. But for those of us called to be ministers and missionaries, we trust in God and our faith called us to continue our work of teaching people about Jesus and about God's way to live.

As I sit here, I wonder when our turn will come, for I think it will. But we will stand together and face whatever is to be our fate, for God is with us, even to the end of time.

* * *

Questions for Contemplation or discussion

1. Do you think it is significant that Priscilla and Acquila are never mentioned separately? What does it say about them as a couple?

2. Why do you think that women in ministry disappeared from the church for so many centuries?

3. What has been your experience of women in ministry? Do they face challenges because they are women?

Dorcas

Acts 9: 36-42

Background

Dorcas is the Greek form of her name, and she was also known as Tabitha, the Aramaic form. She was a disciple, loved by the women of Jaffa where she lived. She performed many charitable works and she is the only woman, according to Scripture, who was raised from the dead by one of the disciples.

* * *

I was very fortunate to live in the port city of Jaffa. It was a beautiful city and prosperous as a trading centre on the coast north of Jerusalem. I was a widow, but very comfortable in my life. I lived in a lovely home well above the water. The breezes blew almost constantly and so it was cool and comfortable. From my roof top I had a wonderful view of the harbour beneath me. I often sat on my roof top to do my sewing and watched the world below me.

For many years, since the death of my husband, I have filled my lonely days making clothing for the widows of this city. Many widows have no one to care for them, and they live a very uncertain life, so I do what I can to help.

An idea came to me one day as I was on my roof top. I was watching people along the beach gathering up anything they could find there. Bits of wood, scraps of cloth, anything that had washed ashore. I realized that I could sit here alone and sew or I could gather some lonely women and we could work together.

And it happened. Most whom I asked were very glad. Glad to have company and to enjoy it on a pleasant roof top. They were also happy. For as widows who were alone, they could do little, however, when we worked together they could offer help to others.

It was a community of friends and co-workers and we became very close as we talked, sewed and shared food together. We became a close-knit community, a sisterhood.

One day I felt very unwell. I thought perhaps I should go to the physician as I was dizzy and weak. I wasn't sure that I could even walk the distance to his home. I decided to see if I would feel better after a little nap, and I lay down on my bed.

When I woke, the room was full of women, and Peter was standing by my bed. I looked about and could see that the women had been crying and Peter looked tired. While I still felt tired, I knew that I was no longer sick the way I had been. I was sitting up and was no longer dizzy or faint. Peter said a farewell blessing and said he had to return to Joppa where he was preaching. With a smile and a wave, he left telling the women to make sure I got some rest.

Tam, one of the talkative women of our group, explained what had happened. They had come as usual for our gathering and found me on my mat. They were sure that I was dead and sent at once for Peter. He came that same day and entered the room where I was lying. Tam said that as they stood outside they could hear him praying.

When I sat up, Peter called the women back onto the room. They all began to rejoice and to praise God. And that is what I saw when I became aware of my room. Some were still crying, but it seemed to me that they were crying in happiness. They brought me some food, broth, cheese, grapes and a honey cake. I sipped the broth and nibbled at the rest and felt much stronger. They ordered me to stay in bed, and they would look after me till I was strong again.

In a few days, I was back on my roof sewing with my friends once more. The group has grown since that day. After the story of my return to life spread in the city, people came to see if it was true. They came out of curiosity, but they stayed because the story was so compelling. They stayed to learn of the one called Jesus and the way he lived.

God does work in strange ways. Very strange ways.

* * *

Questions for Contemplation or Discussion

1. Was this story familiar to you? Have you heard a sermon on this text? Why do you suppose it is not as well known as other miracles?

2. How would you describe her role in the community and what might have been her role in the church?

3. Do you have a woman in your faith journey who was a teacher, mentor and friend? What did she do for you and how did she help you grow in your faith?

Lydia

Acts 16: 11-15, 40

Background

Lydia came from Thyatira and was a seller of dyed goods, specifically purple cloth. She had a home in Philippi and this may have been her main market centre. She was a God fearing woman, and a Jew.

* * *

I was rather unique among women in my time. I owned and ran my own business. I dyed the purple cloth in Thyatira, where I had a home and then sold it in Philippi, a major trading centre. I also owned a home there. Because purple dyes were rare, only the best fabrics were dyed purple, and only the rich could afford my beautiful silks and fine linen goods.

I was a Jew and my faith was important to me. There were few Jews in Philippi and no synagogue. I was a wealthy woman and I had plenty of all the world's goods. But there was an emptiness in my life. To try and fill that need, each Sabbath, a few women, including me, met in a shady spot by the river. There we shared the stories of our history, our God and his dealings with us. We sang the Psalms that we knew and offered our prayers to God.

Women meeting together were always suspect, especially on the Sabbath, so we were alarmed when a group of men approached us. They greeted us in gentle tones and asked if they might speak with us. They sat on the ground beside us and the one named Paul began to talk of a man named Jesus. I was deeply moved by his words and wanted to learn more. I assured him that I kept a proper Jewish home and invited him to be my guest. Before he left Philippi, I had been baptized by him and I became a follower of the way of Jesus, whom Paul called The Christ, the anointed one, the Messiah.

The group by the river grew and soon men were joining us. It was a wonderful time and we grew in our understanding of the new faith and what it meant to live as a follower of Jesus.

When I returned to Thyatira, I wanted to share this wonderful story with people there. I wondered how I could make them understand. I didn't have the eloquent words of Paul, but I knew I needed to share what I had found.

I saw my dyers working with the little shellfish that produced our purple dyes and noticed their hands were stained with the purple colour. They could never get that colour washed off completely. Their hands were changed and I had my connection to speak with them.

I told the people who came to listen, whom I had invited to my house, about the little shellfish that provided our dye. When the shell was opened, the juices of the creature ran out into the bowl we used to catch them in. At first, the juices were clear and colourless, but the moment the sunlight touched the liquid it turned a deep rich purple. Anything that liquid touched instantly became purple.

I said it was like that with God's love. When the sunlight of the presence of the spirit touched our lives, we were changed forever. All those who knew the dyers and the dying business understood my story.

I then told them the stories of Jesus. I spoke of his followers, of the way Jesus treated people and how he loved everyone. Paul said, "In Christ there is no male or female, Jew or Greek, slave or free." He was telling us that we were all beloved of God and forgiven by his mercy. I tried to remember Paul's words and to faithfully pass them on to those who gathered. I took the story back to Philippi too, for to me it explained what happened to us when we let the spirit touch our lives.

As I travelled back and forth between my homes and businesses, both churches were growing and I was able to find leaders to teach while I was away. We gathered to teach, to remember, to learn and to grow in our new faith. We also sang and shared bread together. Sometimes it was a full meal, sometimes a symbolic meal. But in the sharing of bread we remembered Jesus and his death and his resurrection.

* * *

Questions for Contemplation or Discussion

1. Do you think Lydia's business experience would be a help in her ministry? How and why?

2. How difficult is it to live and act as a Christian in the world of commerce and business?

3. What do you see as your ministry within the community of faith?

Amit
Meaning Calm
Mother of Rufus
Mark 15:21
Romans 16:13

Background

The main characters in this story have been by tradition connected as a family. There is no Biblical way this can be proven, but it seems to be logical. Simon, the father, carried Jesus' cross. His sons were Alexander and Rufus and the wife/mother is not named. Paul however, refers to her in his letter to the Romans.

* * *

Our family was in Jerusalem for the Feast of the Passover. We came each year to celebrate with other Jews this high festival in our faith. Our sons were always fascinated by the city and explored it at every opportunity.

They came home one day and talked about a rabbi they had listened to as he spoke to a crowd gathered around him. "He spoke of love, peace and hope, Mother. We want to learn more about him." They saw him again at the temple, with a whip, upsetting the tables and chasing the money-changers out of the temple. My boys were often upset at the cheating they experienced as they changed their money at the temple. I am sure they were cheering this teacher as he chased the dishonest men from their tables.

A few days later we were all in the city, taking in its beauty and grandeur. We heard a great clamour and walked over to the next street. It appeared to be some kind of parade. We could hear people's voices. We heard cheering and jeers and laughter. But I could also hear weeping and crying. The noise of the soldier's feet, marching in rhythm, was very loud, and it is always an ominous sound to us Jews.

As they came closer, the boys cried out, "It is the rabbi." We all watched in disbelief and sorrow, as this man, bleeding and bruised, was stumbling along carrying his cross. As he came in front of us, he fell. Trying to get up as the soldiers whipped him, he fell again. One soldier looked about the crowd and seeing Simon, ordered him to carry the cross. Quickly, Simon whispered to the boys to take me home.

It was many hours later he returned and told us that the teacher had been crucified. Simon told us that his last words were ones of forgiveness for those who had tortured him and put him to death.

As the months went by we learned more about this man called Jesus, and we became believers. We kept many of our Jewish patterns of worship, but we knew that Messiah had come and the world had changed.

Time passed and we learned that Paul, a missionary for the new faith, had been beaten and stoned and had to flee Lystra. His ship arrived in Antioch and my men went to the docks to see him. Simon invited him to come to our home and rest until he became strong again.

I nursed him back to health and we spent many hours listening to his teachings about Jesus. The more we learned the more we knew we had made a good decision to live our lives following the teachings of this man of God, called Jesus. Paul stayed with us for three years and then set out once again to tell the story.

One day we heard the news that a letter had been received from Paul. We all ran to the place where the Christians, as we were now called, gathered. I was overcome with joy when the reader read the letter aloud, and said, "Greetings to Rufus, a chosen servant for Christ, and to his mother, who has been a mother to me."

To know that Paul remembered us, brought me great joy. But even greater joy was the sure knowledge that we were known, loved and forgiven by God. Thanks be to the holy name.

* * *

Questions for Contemplation or Discussion

1. Do you suppose there was fear in this family as Simon was ordered to carry Jesus' cross? Where would that fear come from?

2. How do you think Paul learned about this incident? What do you think he felt as someone who had never met Jesus in person?

3. What does it mean to carry a cross to-day for you?

About the Author
Betty Radford Turcott

Betty trained as a school teacher and furthered her education studying theology, psychology, English Literature and music. She has been the theme speaker for many women's events, one of which was at The Ontario Women's Conference, Waterloo University.

In her talks, she addresses the spiritual journeys of women from the Bible, in history, and her own personal journey. Her passion is reclaiming the material about these women recorded in the Bible and connecting their story with the lives of women of today.

Betty has represented Canadian women at three international events where she shared her spiritual journey and passion for women's stories from the Bible with women from around the world. Many of the stories in this book were inspired and enhanced from listening to and learning from their individual stories. In 2011, she was the Canadian delegate for the World Federation of Methodist Women in Johannesburg.

Betty has a facilitated many workshops with United Church Women, and study groups in various churches of other denominations. She has related her stories of women of the Bible in retreats throughout Ontario and across Canada: British Columbia, Alberta, Manitoba and Newfoundland. She is a planner for her church retreat every fall and often presents the theme.

In addition to Johannesburg, her other international meetings were in Geneva, Jamaica, South Africa, Harare Zimbabwe, and Texas.

And Betty said, "Meeting and sharing stories with women around the world has enriched my life in all aspects of being."

Manufactured by Amazon.ca
Acheson, AB

12473079R00120